NONPROFIT SLEUTHS

Follow the Money

D. LARRY CRUMBLEY
Louisiana State University

GARY GIROUX
Texas A&M University

BOB MEYERS
Free-Lance Writer

1997

When in doubt, tell the truth. It will confound your enemies and astound your friends.
MARK TWAIN

DAME
PUBLICATIONS, INC.
Houston, TX

Cover Design: Developed by Cody Blair

Nonprofit Sleuths is fiction, and except for historical characters, all the characters and adventures are imaginary. Any resemblance to actual persons, living or dead, is purely coincidental.

© **DAME PUBLICATIONS, INC.—1997**
  Houston, TX

All rights reserved. No part of this publication may be reproduced, stored in a retrieval system, or transmitted, in any form or by any means, electronic, mechanical, photocopying, recording, or otherwise, without the prior written permission of the publisher.

ISBN 0-87393-628-0

Printed in the United States of America.

For more information regarding forensic accountants, go to the World Wide Web page at: http://http.tamu.edu:8000/~crumble/forensic/html.

Preface

This supplementary text may be used near the end of the governmental accounting or auditing course. It would be ideal for an MBA program or law school which has light coverage of governmental accounting, or an advanced accounting class which covers governmental accounting. Used in CPA or government training programs would be excellent.

Mix murder, audits, dreams, GAAP, roller coasters, scuba diving, and unrestricted funds together to get an exciting way of learning the governmental accounting process. This suspense thriller format provides a painless way of learning fund concepts, not-for-profit practice and procedure, governmental auditing, and real world examples. This gripping novel puts fund accounting concepts into words a novice can understand and enjoy.

Armed only with pencil, paper, and a compact computer, a new breed of accountants is dispelling the traditional image of their profession as dull bean-counters wearing long-sleeve shirts and green eye-shades. Forensic accountants are the private eyes of the business and governmental worlds. An accountant acts like a watchdog, but a forensic accountant behaves like a bloodhound. They are often used in fraud cases to dissect financial statements and locate hidden assets. Using old-fashioned detective work, Tim and Martin make detection both the art and science that Sherlock Holmes made famous.

Professor Tim Whinney of Ohio University and his friend, Martin Zippa, find the serial murderer in Sherlock Holmes style. Along the way, Martin, a forensic accountant, has his hands full in a governmental audit which involves fraud.

They follow the money trail and use written records to ferret out the guilty parties. Although the book contains educational materials, key words, appendices, questions and problems, the plot is a page turner.

A novel is a flexible teaching tool to overcome boredom in the classroom. The concepts and attitudes a novel teaches last long after the facts are gone, since something a student feels internally stays with him or her much longer than cold, hard facts.

Comments from readers are welcomed.

NONPROFIT SLEUTHS: FOLLOW THE MONEY

Table of Contents

Preface

	Page	
Chapter 1		1
Chapter 2		5
Chapter 3		14
Chapter 4		22
Chapter 5		29
Chapter 6		34
Chapter 7		39
Chapter 8		44
Chapter 9		51
Chapter 10		57
Chapter 11		74
Chapter 12		78
Chapter 13		84
Chapter 14		91
Chapter 15		97
Chapter 16		101
Chapter 17		108
Chapter 18		115
Chapter 19		119
Chapter 20		122
Chapter 21		129
Chapter 22		136
Chapter 23		141
Chapter 24		148
Chapter 25		151
Chapter 26		155
Chapter 27		161
Chapter 28		169
Appendices		179
Appendix 1 - Auditor's Report		180
Appendix 2 - Types of Financial Audits of State & Local Governments		181
Appendix 3 - Key Terms		182
Review Questions		183
Multiple Choice		184

v

Chapter One

A governmental accounting system must make it possible both: (a) to present fairly and with full disclosure the financial position and results of financial operations of the funds and account groups of the governmental accounting principles, and (b) to determine and demonstrate compliance with finance-related legal and contractual provisions.
                          The National Council on
                          Governmental Accounting

"Night after night, the same terrifying dream, and the ending never varies--the man murders me."

"And the violence at the end is quite graphic?"

"That's putting it mildly," Tim Whinney confirmed to his close friend and fellow faculty member, Justin O'Malley. "The gun cracks once, and I feel the bullet sinking into my heart. I can literally feel my pulse coming to a stop. Then the gun cracks again, and I can almost trace the second bullet's slow flight through my brain. The impact is pushing me backwards, and my last thought...is that I'm sinking into a pool of bright, red blood. Somehow I know that there won't be any other thoughts...because I'm dead."

O'Malley, a professor of psychology, leaned back in his chair and gave the matter some consideration. "You've had this dream for seven nights in a row?"

"That's right. And I want to get rid of it."

"I can imagine. Does it frighten you enough to wake you up each time?"

"Usually. And then it takes me quite a while to get back to sleep."

"You kill weeds at their roots, Tim. You need to find out what's causing this dream."

"But that's just it. Nothing's been bothering me, Justin. No one's made any threats against me. I don't even have any bill collectors chasing me."

"I envy you there. Well, let's see. You're not up for tenure for quite a long while. Any problems around the house? Major repairs?"

"I rent. And, I've been spending most of my weekends at my uncle and aunt's farm. They're about eighty miles east of here, on the Ohio River."

"Is that right? Has the flooding threatened them?"

"I called Uncle Everett last night, and he said it's nip and tuck. But they're not moving out yet."

"Hmmm." O'Malley slowly rubbed his chin. "You know, Tim, sometimes a cluster of little things can knock around in your subconscious, and nag at you. We'd all like to lead worry-free lives, but let's be honest. Things go wrong. Milk sours, and dreams can become nightmares. In your case, I'm sure you're concerned about your uncle's home being flooded. And worrying about tenure or not yet having it could be a factor."

"But seven nights in a row? And each night more forceful?"

"You've heard of a stalled weather system, haven't you? A sinister explanation is hardly mandatory. Look...take a slow-paced, restful break over the Memorial weekend. Go out on a date. If you're not better by Tuesday, then your next step should be a complete exam by a doctor. There might be a simple physiological cause."

Tim was somewhat surprised by the tone of finality in his colleague's last sentence. The tall young professor rose from his chair, but was reluctant to leave. "Justin, what about the rest of the dream," Tim said with some insistence. "What about the colors? And the symbols?"

"They always mean different things to different people. Believe me, the more you think about it, the more likely you'll dream it again. Shelve it. Take a three-day vacation. And don't forget, you need to write the new regression results on audit delays so we can send the paper to the *Journal of Accounting and Public Policy*."

"I know. And speaking of publishing, I've had a major article accepted in the *Accounting Review*."

"Splendid. Is that the project on audit quality in the public sector that you presented at the annual American Accounting Association meeting last year?"

"That's the one. The paper really supports low balling practices by auditors. In the year of an auditor change, fees are much lower and audit hours higher than in subsequent years."

"What an amazing results. Does that mean the auditors lose money the first year?"

"Probably," said Tim. "They make it up in future years since auditor changes aren't that common. What's even stranger is that audit quality goes down after several years."

"How can you measure audit quality?"

"Under the Single Audit Act state and local governmental audits are reviewed by federal and state agencies. The school district audits I was studying were reviewed by the state education agency. We analyzed the review letters and came up with an audit quality score for each audit."

"So, I guess that's what they call auditing the auditor."

"Right again," laughed Tim.

Tim thanked his friend for the time and advice rendered, then headed across the campus on the brick walks. All the walks and buildings on campus were made of brick. At one time the Hocking River ran through the campus and caused severe flooding in the spring. The river was rerouted in 1969. A clap of thunder marked the beginning of an afternoon rainstorm.

Copeland Hall is on the corner of Court Street and President Street. A unique feature of the campus is that some of it is intertwined with the town of Athens. Baron's Men's Shop is just a few steps from Copeland Hall, which houses the School of Business.

Once he was safely inside Copeland Hall, Tim stopped by his mailbox in the accounting department on the third floor, and eagerly ripped open a letter postmarked from Chicago. The handwritten missive was from his best friend, Martin Zippa.

> Dear Tim,
>
> I received your letter yesterday.
>
> Yes, as I explained in my last letter, I'm coming your way. I hope to perform an audit on your fine city of Greenharbor. Expect to see me at your uncle's farm on the 31st. I'll take your map with me.
>
> I wish you already had firm plans for the summer. We'll talk about that when I get there. If you really think you can stand me for two weeks, I'll stay.
>
> By the way, our money from the drug sales that I laundered and invested has now doubled. See you soon,
>
> Martin

Doing a double take of the last sentence, Tim quickly checked to be sure no one else had glimpsed the closing words. What a stupid idea to put that in writing. Nonetheless, it was good to hear from Martin, and good to know they would be together again.

Twenty feet away, the senior secretary in the accounting department caught sight of the dark-haired, attractive professor. "Oh Dr. Whinney! A message for you!"

Folding and pocketing Martin's letter, Tim ambled over to her desk. "What's new, Olivia?"

"I took a message for you. Let's see...where did I ..." Beginning to shuffle through the stack of notes before her, she drifted into a well-worn sidepath. "Professor, did I ever tell you how much you remind me of my cousin, Harold? Such a handsome fellow, and I swear you have his eyes...a cornflower blue, I always called them."

"Yes, you've mentioned that. At least once or twice. Uh, while you're looking for that message, I'll just..."

"Here it is!" Triumphantly brandishing a brief note, Olivia adjusted her glasses and provided an interpretation of her inimitable shorthand.

"The gist of what your aunt said: 'Come home immediately. Don't wait. A dead man's body was found in our barn. Your uncle is being treated as a suspect. Your help urgently needed.'"

Olivia returned Tim's open-mouthed stare with a look of mild puzzlement. "Not the happiest of messages, wouldn't you say?"

Chapter Two

A fund is defined as a fiscal and accounting entity with a self-balancing set of accounts recording cash and other financial resources, together with all related liabilities and residual equities or balances, and changes therein, which are segregated for the purpose of carrying on specific activities or attaining certain objectives in accordance with special regulations, restrictions, or limitations.
                    Government Accounting Standards Board

Tim's first move was to try telephoning his uncle and aunt. But a connection could not be made, and the operator offered an explanation that the most recent rainstorms had aggravated flood conditions and cut off most telephone service to Greenharbor and other towns along the hardest hit portion of the Ohio River.

Hurriedly Tim packed his briefcase, realizing that his plans to see an evening movie on campus would have to be canceled. He glanced across the hall and saw Dr. Vince Corbett.

"Hey Vince, you headed for West Virginia this weekend to see your girlfriend?"

"Well I sure don't plan to spend Memorial weekend at Ohio University. What a bummer." Ohio University, founded in 1804, was the first institution of higher learning in the old Northwest Territory. The 17,000 student campus is located in Athens, Ohio, about 75 miles from Columbus.

"Yeah...but are you leaving anytime soon? I'm a bit desperate for a ride to Greenharbor. My car is having its transmission rebuilt."

"Oh...I suppose I could go the northern route...if none of those hellacious old roads are under water."

"Let's try it. My uncle and aunt have a problem, and they want me there."

"All right. Want to leave in about thirty minutes?"

"Sure. Thanks, Vince."

Tim used the intervening time to review his scheduling book. He had one remaining exam to give next Tuesday, and that would conclude his third year at Ohio University.

After picking up their suitcases, they headed eastward on U.S. 50. Tim noted the dark clouds gathering in the east, and wondered how much longer his uncle's farm would be safe from the flood.

"What do you hear from Martin?" Vince asked, bringing Tim's thoughts to another problem.

"He wrote me. I guess he'll be down next week from Chicago...to visit me at my uncle's farm. And he also has an accounting engagement in Greenharbor."

"I'd like to see him again."

"Everybody liked Martin." A wistful smile crossed Tim's face.

"What's he doing in Chicago?" Vince asked.

"He's working for a small CPA firm. Actually, he says many of the smaller practitioners are becoming investigative accountants. He calls himself a forensic accountant."

"Why?"

"Apparently the big-six CPA firms are becoming more and more competitive with the smaller firms."

"In other words, the big-six are taking more and more of their business," Vince interjected.

"Probably. Anyway, Martin is trying to specialize in audits of governmental and nonprofit organizations." Tim shifted to a different position in the passenger's seat. "Governments are subject to financial and compliance audits based upon generally accepted governmental auditing standards -- GAGAS, in accounting jargon. Nonprofit organizations are subject to financial audits, similar to commercial firms, but with unique requirements based upon organization type. Colleges and universities also are subject to single audit requirements if they receive federal funds."

"So they're sort of like Quincy, the guy in the T.V. series several years ago?"

"Yes. Martin says these forensic guys get involved with fraud and bankruptcy situations. They look beyond the books and records and actually dig into the body."

"Now, let's see. You and Martin graduated from Ohio State University together. You went off to the University of Illinois for a Ph.D., and Martin went into the real world. You wound up at OU. Any regrets?"

"No, but I'd like to do some expert witnessing myself."

"Forget it until you finish more first tier research articles and obtain tenure. Then you can look at the real world."

They drove in silence for a few minutes. Then Vince said, "I'm thinking about buying some bonds from my home town."

"Wow. I didn't know they paid so much in the Marketing Department. You need tax-exempt income?"

"Not that much. But royalties have been good on my three books. I'm in the 31% federal tax bracket and state income taxes may be going up. Besides, I'd like to support my home town. Do cities ever go bankrupt?"

"It's possible. Bankruptcy of commercial firms is common, but bankruptcy of governments has been rare since the 1930's. But some communities have filed for Chapter 9 bankruptcy. At least 16 states specifically grant municipalities the authority to fight for bankruptcy. Remember Orange County? They speculated in derivatives."

"How do I check out my town?"

"Check the bond rating first. Most municipalities have investment grade rating, BAA or higher. Then, check the interest rate; it should be similar to other bonds with the same rating and maturity."

"Well," said Vince, "it's just a small town; I'm pretty sure the bonds don't have a rating."

"Then you have work to do: a thorough financial analysis of the town. The comprehensive annual financial report and operating budget of your town may provide useful information for detecting impending hardship. You should be able to determine if the city is in a chronic stage."

"Read the Director of Finance's letter on operations. That will give you a general idea on what the town is doing. Then turn to the operating statement of the General Fund and see if the town has a surplus or deficit. Then, go to the statistical section at the and of the annual report for 10-year trend data...."

"Whoa," shouted Vince. "Remember, I barely know the difference between a debit and a credit."

"Sorry. I got carried away. Get a set of statements and bring them over and we'll calculate some financial ratios and compare them to averages for similar cities. Any questions?"

"Are cities required to have their financial statements audited?" Vince asked.

"Governments are subject to financial and compliance audits based on generally accepted governmental auditing standards. The Single Audit Act includes significant additional federal regulations for state and local governments," Tim said.

"Single Audit Act," Vince repeated.

"The Single Audit Act requires every state or local government receiving $100,000 or more in federal financial assistance in a fiscal year to have a single audit annually. State or local governments receiving at least $25,000 in assistance may have a single audit or a series of separate grant audits. Governments receiving less than $25,000 are exempt from single audit requirements, but must maintain records of administration of federal financial assistance they receive. Martin wants the contract to audit

Greenharbor."

"Are you going to help?"

"I hope so. I need the money," Tim smiled.

"What are the audit objectives under this Single Audit Act?" Vince inquired.

"They are associated with financial statements, internal control and compliance. The auditor must determine if financial statements are prepared according to GAAP. Internal control systems should be established to provide reasonable assurance that federal funds are used in compliance with applicable laws. Also, the state and local governments must comply with regulations that may have a material effect on each major federal assistance program." Tim paused to catch his breath.

"Three separate types of audit reports are required to confirm these three audit objectives. *First*, a report on the examination of the basic financial statements and the schedule of federal financial assistance is required. *Second*, a report on internal accounting controls based on the auditor's evaluation is required. The report is based on both the evaluation of internal control as part of the financial audit and an evaluation based on the Single Audit Act and related federal regulations. *Third*, a report on compliance with federal laws and regulations for each major federal assistance program, for non-major federal programs, and for the entity's compliance with laws and regulations in general is required. Major weaknesses in internal controls and material noncompliance with federal regulation require written reports to both government officials and cognizant audit agencies."

"Enough! Enough!" Vince almost shouted. "Accountants are dull. If I find financial statements from my hometown, what type of ratios should I calculate?"

"Now that you have sufficiently offended me, why should I answer?" Tim paused.

"The basic categories are liquidity, leverage, performance, turnover characteristics, and fiscal stress. Liquidity can be measured with the current ratios of the General Fund. Current assets divided by current liabilities, which analyzes the ability of an organization to meet short-term obligations as they come due. Leverage measures deal with the use of debt. Debt per capita is a good place to start. Revenue divided by expenditures of the General Fund is a good performance measure. A ratio of one is a balanced budget, below one is a deficit. If deficits are common, that's bad news and you need more analysis. Demographic characteristics should be considered in measuring fiscal stress, such as population changes, unemployment rate, and per capita income."

As they passed through the small town of Coolville, Vince changed the subject. "Have you made any sense out of Olivia's message?"

"Not really. It sounds so weird that I can't help wondering if she didn't get her wires crossed completely. There's no way I could see my uncle as a suspect in a murder case."

"I've said hello to him and your aunt a couple of times. They're run-of-the-mill, pleasant farming folks." Vince nudged Tim's shoulder. "Isn't that what you *really* wanted to be in life, Tim? Just an educated farm boy in overalls? Fess up, now."

"Why do you think I left Indiana? I'd rather be dead than plowing a field or drudging on a humdrum repetitive job for a living. I want some excitement out of life."

"Teaching governmental accounting in Athens, Ohio, with a population of 12,000?"

"It has its moments. Don't forget our annual Halloween bash. On the Saturday nearest Halloween, there is a huge party in downtown Athens. Students from colleges throughout Ohio, Indiana, Kentucky, Michigan, West Virginia, and the world descend upon our town to have a good time. Last year the crowd was around 25,000 and there were some exceptional costumes. There were only 237 arrests."

"Wow. Next you'll tell me that our kelly green and white football team will win a game in Peden Stadium."

"Well, our mascot bobcat is great, and the half-time show by the Marching One-Ten is supreme."

"So that's why most of the students leave after the half-time show." Vince smiled.

Their journey turned northward as they left Marietta on Ohio Route 7. They moved ever closer to the ominous cloudbank that seemed to be preparing a Neptunian attack on the swollen Ohio River Valley.

Continuing northeastward on Ohio Route 7 at the eastern edge of the state, Vince drove through the small town of Fly and then on to Greenharbor. One mile north of Greenharbor, the Buick slowed to make a right turn onto a narrow county road that connected the Whinney house and five others to the state highway.

"You don't have to take me all the way to my doorstep, Vince. Hey, slow down...looks like water over the road."

A sheriff's cruiser was parked at a low point where several inches of water covered all but the west edge of the asphalt roadway, which Tim's uncle and his neighbors called the Old Nelson Road. Vince rolled his window down and chatted with the raincoat-wrapped deputy.

"It's even worse at the north end of the loop," the deputy reported. "We're only letting residents in."

"My friend here lives just up the road. At the Whinney farm."

"Oh...yes. Everett and Mildred Whinney, up at the Old Nelson Place. Quite a stir, the way they found Sid Burk's body this morning." Water dripped off the deputy's cap as he looked across the front seat. "Are you their son?"

"Nephew."

"Well, you'd best go on up. I think you can still get around the big puddle here. I'll need both your names, though. Somethin' to do with a list of murder suspects."

After the two professors produced driver's licenses for identification, Vince made his way gingerly around the floodwater.

It was less than a mile from the low place in the loop road to the Whinney driveway. Normally at this point the old roadway was the halfway mark between Route 7 on the west and the Ohio River to the east. But, under present conditions, the loop was only a few feet from the expanded river.

"Won't your house have water in it?" Vince asked as he cautiously turned into the drive.

"No, it's on a small rise, like the old barn."

"Who's Sid Burk?"

"Well, he *was* our neighbor on the north. I hardly knew him. A quiet fellow."

"He'll be even quieter now, if you'll forgive the irreverence."

"Your sensitivity to human tragedy is one of your most endearing qualities, Vince."

"I would have made a good lawyer."

The rain began to descend more forcefully as Tim stepped out of the mud-covered Buick and extracted a suitcase. "Won't you come in?"

"With all due thanks, I'd better get out of here before my car floats over to West Virginia. I'd love to hear about the murder, but it's already getting late and I need to be home. If I don't see you next Tuesday, call or visit me."

"I sure will, Vince. Thanks for the ride."

* * *

Inside the Whinney farmhouse, Tim greeted his uncle, his aunt and Sheriff Don Kruger, with whom Tim had discussed several legal points in the preparation of a term paper for a business law course several years ago. Tim embraced the hope that the sheriff considered him a friend.

Aunt Mildred was profuse with apologies for not having heard her nephew's arrival or helping him cart his belongings inside. A dark-haired woman of fifty-two, she was slim, plain and peppery, but Tim admired her deeply for her courage and her principles.

Uncle Everett seemed preoccupied with his own thoughts. A dedicated farmer who performed all tasks with the least amount of exertion possible, he was fifty-six and hearty, but certain to be deferential where a police investigation was involved.

Tim's uncle and aunt, his cherished relatives who had been a second---and generally more indulgent---set of parents to him, were a transplanted portion of his family who had moved to Ohio less than two years ago to build a new future. Were their lives---as well as their rain-soaked farm---on the brink of disaster?

For his answer, the young man turned toward Sheriff Kruger, who was jotting some notes on a clipboard. Hard-working, efficient, jovial only when political events demanded it, the forty-one-year-old sheriff had shown some admirable skills. Tim wondered if he would still admire the man when the current investigation was over.

"Sheriff Kruger, my curiosity is about ready to burst. All I know is that our neighbor, Sid Burk, is dead---apparently murdered. What happened?"

The sheriff put down his pencil. "Doc, your uncle went to his barn early this morning, and found a body lying beneath the loose hay on the floor. Mr. Burk had been shot once in the head with a .38 slug, which the coroner recovered. Based on the evidence, Burk was shot somewhere else and transported here. The man died yesterday afternoon."

"I see. But how does any of that cast suspicion on my uncle?"

"Basically, it doesn't. I've told your uncle and your aunt that they are not under suspicion."

"But on the contrary," Aunt Mildred inserted, "your chief deputy, Wade Nagle, made some very distinct remarks that there had to be a reason for the body to be on our farm, and therefore we had to know something that we weren't telling."

"Which is pure rubbish," Uncle Everett spoke up. "Like I said, once or twice I chatted with the man across our fence, but I didn't know him beyond that, and had no dealings with him."

"I'm sure our routine investigation will reinforce what you're saying," the sheriff retorted.

"I got the impression from the deputy down the way that there may be some suspects."

"Right Doc...or can I call you Tim?"

"Sure," Tim answered. "I'm an accounting prof, not a medical doctor."

"Tim, by a strange turn of events the flood itself has given us a short but comprehensive list of suspects."

"What do you mean?"

The sheriff shifted to a more relaxed position. "Somebody murdered Burk yesterday afternoon and moved him here before seven a.m. today. There are some very washed-out car tracks by your uncle's old gray haybarn. So, we can reasonably conclude that the murderer brought the body here by car, late yesterday or early this morning. For two days the Old Nelson Road has been cut off by high water on the north and dangerously close to it on the south. We've had a deputy at that southern low spot, where you came in, since Wednesday night. To make sure only local residents and their guests came into your water-ringed peninsula, we've checked licenses and recorded the names of whoever drove in or out. The murderer had to go through the checkpoint, possibly with the corpse in his trunk. There's no other way in."

"But Burk lived next door, he might have..."

"The sheriff's right," Uncle Everett said. "Those tire tracks weren't mine, and they couldn't have been made very long ago."

"So, ruling out the unlikely combination of canoe, wheelbarrow and phony tire tracks, we have a complete list of all possible suspects."

"Unless someone had false ID."

"But we've located each person, and there are no strangers wearing wigs." Sheriff Kruger pulled a sheet of paper from his clipboard.

"Would you like to know who the possibilities are?"

"I'd love to."

"I thought this might catch your interest. First of all, of the six houses in here, only you Whinneys and the Grants were home. Four other people drove in, for one reason or another. Verna Barger, the real estate lady; Novia Dixon, our local theater director; Ling Sumoto, a businessman in Greenharbor; and one out-of-towner, a Walter Rankin, who was on vacation and apparently looking for some fishing spot."

"Hmmm. That's an unusual list."

Just then Deputy Nagle popped in the front door without knocking, and stepped toward the sheriff. Nagle was thirty-eight, ambitious and often caustic.

"Deputy, did you find anything of significance in Sid Burk's house?"

"I certainly did." The deputy cast a jaundiced eye at Uncle Everett. "Mr. Whinney, I thought you told us you had never been inside Mr. Burk's house."

"That's right. I never have."

Another deputy stepped inside, carrying a timeworn toolbox with old lettering on it. The name Everett Whinney was faintly legible.

"Then *how*," Deputy Nagle demanded, "do you explain this toolbox in Burk's kitchen?" To the sheriff he added, "I think we have grounds enough to arrest Everett Whinney for murder."

Chapter Three

A billion here, a billion there; soon it adds up to real money.
                              Senator Everett Dirksen

   As looks of surprise and dismay began to multiply, Tim was the first to find his voice. "Hold it, hold it!" Everyone turned toward the room's youngest occupant. "Sheriff, as I can tell you, and as my aunt can tell you, that old toolbox has been sitting for months in the red barn where we keep most of the farming equipment. There's no lock on that barn. Anybody, *anybody in the world*, could have moved that box to another location. How could you possibly charge someone with a serious felony on the basis of such unpersuasive evidence?"
   "And just *how* did this toolbox come to be in the murder victim's house?" Deputy Nagle demanded again.
   "I have no idea," Uncle Everett replied.
   "Maybe, for some odd reason," Aunt Mildred interjected, seeming to make up the thought as she went along, "Mr. Burk needed some tools, and took them while Everett and I were gone---probably meaning to return them right away."
   "Yes, that's a charitable possibility," Tim agreed. "But I can think of a more pragmatic answer. Perhaps Sid Burk was a thief. That would explain the toolbox, plus give us a motive for his murder---one of his victims decided to draw the final curtain on Burk's rapaciousness. Placing his body in our barn was therefore meant to confuse the situation by directing suspicion toward an innocent bystander. By the way, was the toolbox dusted for prints?"
   "Come on guys," Sheriff Kruger chided, "that old rust bucket wouldn't hold prints."
   Several moments of silence passed, and Tim began to wonder if his spirited defense had accomplished its purpose. His only consolation was that Nagle was more subdued in tone and volume when he delivered his next salvo.
   "Funny how this greedy thief didn't have any other stolen goods in his house."
   The sheriff drummed his fingers on the living room mantle. "Well, that just points out how many unanswered questions and unexamined suspects we have. But, let's call it quits for tonight. I suspect most of us are frazzled. I know I am."
   Sheriff Kruger reached for his hat, his customary

signal that a questioning session should end. "A good arrest needs evidence, and we don't have that yet. So let's adjourn."

The sheriff made his way to the front door, then turned and waited for his two deputies. Nagle frowned menacingly at the Whinneys, then stalked out of the house. The other deputy set the box on the floor and left.

"Good night, folks," the sheriff concluded pleasantly enough as he closed the front door behind him.

"Well, you can see what we've had to put up with all day," Aunt Mildred told her nephew after a short pause to insure the departure of the law officers. "We'll be lucky if we can make it through the night without Nagle finding some other piece of flimsy evidence and arresting us in our bedclothes."

"I think he's more intent on arresting *me*," Uncle Everett added. "Probably thinks it would be unlikely for a woman to use a .38."

"But certainly not impossible," Tim said. "Why don't we calmly and carefully go over everything that's happened today."

"What good will that do?" Aunt Mildred asked.

"It'd help me with my own investigation."

"Mildred, we need all the help we can get."

"Yes Everett, I understand. But Tim, there's something *you'd* better understand. A man was murdered, and at least two things have been done by the murderer to shift the blame on us, the newest residents in the area. If you go interfering with his plans, what might happen to you?"

* * *

Tim spent a restless night in his bedroom, waking every two or three hours as thunder and lightning interrupted his sleep. But he might not have slept well anyway, in view of the many problems and decisions ahead. He was proud of himself for having kept his mouth shut. He had almost answered his aunt by saying "Well I'm sure that I'm not going to die, the way I keep dreaming I will, night after night..." That had almost popped out, but he had caught himself in time.

Martin was coming, and their summer plans needed to be discussed. But with this murder there might be a roadblock to making plans. Money...work...suspects...and dreams. Tim wanted to get a full night's rest, yet he dreaded the development that deep sleep had brought him the past seven nights in a row.

He didn't want to go through that again. The candle, the search, the monk, the white fruit, the crows, the man named Midnight. And, of course, that horrible ending. Being shot. Dying.

A flash of lightning illuminated the sky outside his window, and Tim glanced at his bedside clock. Four a.m. Dream or no dream, he needed some sleep. "I'll tell Martin; I'll tell him everything."

At eight thirty, he awoke to a clear Saturday with sunshine. He had not experienced the dream. That alone was an energizing start for the day.

He dressed and ate breakfast, pleased to hear his uncle's report that the water had risen only six inches overnight. With a clearing trend predicted, the worst of the flooding might be over.

Borrowing his uncle's car, a ten-year-old Chevrolet, Tim drove to the sheriff's office in Greenharbor, hoping to talk with Sheriff Kruger.

"I had a feeling you might drop by, Tim. I also have a feeling that by now you've thought it all over, and concluded that you ought to do some investigating on your own."

"You're a perceptive man. If you were in my place, would you wring your hands and do nothing?"

"No, I suppose not." The sheriff's voice changed to his straight-from-the-shoulder tone. "I've thought about ways to discourage you, but the bottom line seems to be that there aren't any. You're bright, you're eager, and you no doubt see your uncle and aunt as being victimized. All right---let's not waste time and energy trying to climb past each other. June's nearly here. I've told Deputy Nagle that he's got the full month of June to investigate and give me his report."

"Nagle? Is he the best you've got?"

"Basically, yes. He needs a little something...just now...to fill his spare time. But, I'll give you the same thirty days. Go snoop around, and see what you can learn. But keep in mind that you have no more authority than any other citizen. If someone says 'I'm tired of your questions and get out of my house,' that's what you'll have to do. Tact and caution could prove to be your two best friends."

"But if Nagle and I have the same territory, won't our efforts be redundant?"

"I don't think so. I'm asking you to respect his right to investigate. If you do, then he has been informed that he must respect your personal efforts. Frankly, I think your dual approaches will serve me the way a pair of human eyes serve the brain---the same target, but slightly different perspectives. Yours will have an academic, research flavor, and his will be more procedural. He has to assume eight suspects, and you're assuming six. It'll make a difference."

Tim realized he was getting a better deal than he had any right to expect. "When does all of this start?"

"Two p.m. today. I just called your aunt and uncle, and they're waiting for you to get back with the car so they can attend the inquest."

* * *

Promptly at two, Tim returned to the county law enforcement building. In one of the meeting rooms, Sheriff Kruger sat at the head of an oblong table. To his left was the aged coroner with a notepad and recorder. To his right was Deputy Nagle. In addition to Uncle Everett and Aunt Mildred, five other people sat in chairs around the room.

"We'll do this very informally," the sheriff intoned as if he were trying to make a child believe that dentistry was truly painless. "No one's on trial here, and we appreciate your coming on such short notice. With Monday being a holiday, we wanted to get moving. Today worked out satisfactorily for everyone except Elston Grant, who's in the middle of trying a case up in Cleveland. But we'll hear from him before long, and we'll all meet again if we need to. First, the coroner's report."

The coroner gave a brief and unenlightening statement. Then the sheriff picked up the ball, mentioning that Burk's death was now more closely established. "At four p.m. Thursday, someone shot him to death. The physical evidence clearly points to his body being dragged from a car trunk to the floor of Mr. Whinney's haybarn. By now, all of you know that the road north of the Whinney farm was completely cut off by water, as of last Wednesday. Now folks, we've checked the houses, the cars, and the terrain, and there's only one way to look at it. Only eight human beings went in, came out, or were staying there. Only eight. Therefore, one of the eight is the murderer. Now I don't suppose anybody here would care to confess, and save me a lot of time and trouble?"

Total silence.

The sheriff cleared his throat. "Never an extrovert when you need one. All right, let's go over the facts." He directed everyone's attention to a large map of the area in question.

"Going from south to north, there are six houses. The first is owned by the Shumways, who are on an extended vacation. They weren't there, and had no vehicles on their property. The second house is the Old Nelson Place, now owned by the Whinneys. Mr. and Mrs. Whinney made a total of three trips in and out, and they are with us today. Mr. Whinney, you own an old pickup that won't run and a Chevrolet sedan, is that right?"

"Yes."

"Any chance someone could have stolen or used either vehicle Thursday night?"

"None. The pickup's dead, and the car was inside the garage, only a stone's throw from our bedroom window. *Locked* inside."

"Okay. Proceeding north, the next driveway is to the late Sid Burk's house. Mr. Burk's car was being repaired on Thursday, at a Greenharbor car dealership. He never picked it up, and now we know why.

"The fourth property is Orick Farm, and no one has been there since Mrs. Orick's death in March. The fifth place is Sparlin Farm, and since the Sparlins died...it's been three or four years now...only their son has lived there. He's out of town, and his cousin says he'll be back next week. Again, no cars there.

"The last possibility is the Grant house. Elston Grant the attorney passed our checkpoint, going home, at three p.m. on Thursday.

He drove out, apparently going to the airport for his trip to Cleveland, on Friday morning. He shares the house with his nephew, Douglas, who's with us today. Mr. Grant, you passed our checkpoint at three-thirty on Thursday afternoon, left that evening, returned home very early Friday morning, and then left again about nine a.m. Are you as certain as Mr. Whinney that no one could've stolen or borrowed your car?"

Douglas Grant was a handsome young man of twenty-six, nearly Tim's height with a similar build and coloring. "That just wouldn't be possible. My uncle and I keep our cars in the garage next to the house. There's even a burglar alarm there. So I'm sure no one tampered with Uncle Elston's car, or mine."

"Very well. Let's hear from the four other people who entered the area after Thursday morning."

"But you said the man died at four p.m.," objected a middle-aged man with sharp features and sandy brown hair.

"Just a little shorthand, Mr. Rankin. Any car that entered the area is suspect, but there were only eight of you, all together, taking it from Wednesday. Since Burk was alive Thursday morning, when he dropped his car off, we might as well take it from Thursday morning forward. Now why were you there, Mr. Rankin?"

"I'm in town on a business trip. Planning to look at refurbishing an old amusement park with some other people, a few miles south of here. I drove out Thursday to check on the fishing site where Nelson Creek meets the Ohio."

"But that's on private property, and there hasn't been any good fishing in Nelson Creek for years."

"Well, obviously I got stuck with *old* information."

"Obviously. And *you*, Miss Dixon? Why would the director of the Greenharbor Little Theater be entering a flooded farming area?"

"That's easily explained," replied the tall, attractive blonde. Now thirty-six, she had been working with a small group of dedicated local performers for the past ten years. "I went there to get a check from Mr. Sumoto, who is a stalwart supporter of our theater group. Kindly note that I arrived there well after the time when you say this man died."

"That's quite correct. Your *car* entered the area at five forty-five. Whether you had *walked* into the area at four p.m. is unknown. Or his body could have been in your car trunk."

"My goodness! *Anyone* could have walked there."

"Yes, that's true. But the killer, or else his knowing accomplice, had to have a car to move the body. Can anyone vouch for your whereabouts at four p.m.?"

"Is that some sort of accusation?"

"No ma'am. This is just a friendly inquest," the sheriff returned with a smile. "Now as for you, Mr. Sumoto, would you care to authenticate Miss Dixon's story?"

The dignified businessman of Japanese heritage seldom showed any expression on his face or in his voice. At fifty-two, Ling Sumoto was a respected member of the Greenharbor business community. "She is telling you the truth. There was some urgency in her getting this check to the bank by Friday morning, so she called my office, found out where I was, and drove out to the Orick place."

"I see. And why were *you* at Orick Farm?"

"To inspect it closely, and to meet Mrs. Barger there. Rumor had it that the property was coming on the market at a very favorable price."

"Then it would appear, Mr. Sumoto, that you and Mrs. Barger were together from about three p.m. to six p.m. At Orick Farm, that is---a very short walk from Sid Burk's house."

Verna Barger, widow and real estate saleswoman, stuck a pencil into the jet black hair that she kept raked into a bun behind her head. At forty-eight, she held a reputation for tartness and shrewdness. "My turn at last, is it? Very well, let's not beat around the bush. I was there, at Orick Farm, because I represent the owner. Yes, Mr. Sumoto was there, chasing a bargain like a bloodhound after a convict. But there had been a misunderstanding about the sale price, and when I finally got that point across, it seemed to turn Mr. Sumoto's sweet pickles to dill, if you catch my drift. I had some straightening up to do, and he felt inclined to check out the barn and fences. So, we were *not* together at four p.m. We were *not* in constant view of each other, and I can't say who shot who. But I didn't do it. My pistol is a .22, and even that hurts my ears. If this fool shoots a .38 very often, I'd look for him at a hearing aid store."

"Thank you for your candor, Mrs. Barger. I know that some of you are eager to get on with your Memorial Day plans, so I won't keep you. I don't think any magic solutions will appear today. But either I or Deputy Nagle will be talking to each of you soon. Good day."

Tim sized up what he had learned, and decided he had best try to draw out Mr. Rankin more thoroughly. As an out-of-town resident, his availability might soon be over. Also, of the seven who were present, Rankin's explanation for being near Burk's property was the weakest.

As soon as the sheriff stepped out of the room, the others began milling about and discussing various aspects of the investigation. As Tim made his way across the room toward Rankin, he realized that the common oral theme was each person's innocence.

"I certainly didn't have..."
"It's unthinkable that I..."
"What sense does it make to suggest I..."

Logical reactions, Tim thought. Regretfully, the next step would be to whisper shadowy theories of who *was* guilty. Then the principle of least resistance would be followed. Who was the least well known, the newest resident, and the one whose barn had become the corpse's resting place?

Somewhat like the purchase method for treating inventory in a government unit. Under this approach an inventory item is charged directly to the expenditure account of the department purchasing the item. Thus, the item is completely charged to the expenditure account no matter when the inventory item is actually used. Even under the purchase method, however, if there is any inventory on hand at the end of the year, an entry debits inventory and credits a reserve for inventory.

    Tim was on the verge of telling Rankin that a person was innocent until proven guilty when Deputy Nagle cut between them.
    "Mr. Rankin, do you suppose that we could meet..."
    Tim frowned, and took a step backwards. Would he be outmaneuvered at every point by the "official" investigator? Would Nagle go out of his way to deal duds and blanks to others, while hogging the ace draws for himself?
    "Oh, Professor..."
    The young professor turned and looked toward Sheriff Kruger. "Phone call."
    "Someone calling me *here*? Who is it?" Tim asked.
    "She didn't give a name. But she's got a sexy voice."

Chapter Four

Financial disclosures were found to be associated with factors representing cross-sectional differences in the signaling and monitoring incentives of municipal officials. In addition, evidence was found to suggest that increased financial disclosure is associated with a measure of auditor reputation. Specifically, an index composed of disclosures which at the time were required under GAAP was found to be significantly related to audit fees for a sample of U.S. municipalities.

Paul A. Copley

Tim picked up the phone. "Tim Whinney."

"Yes, Dr. Whinney, this is Lisa Flinn. Remember me?"

"Oh...Lisa...it's good to hear from you."

"Well I certainly haven't been hearing much of anything from you. I thought we were going to get together for lunch today."

"Oh...that's right...I told you I'd be back from OU by noon at the latest, and we were supposed to talk about...the summer."

"That's the way it was...and needless to say, Lyda's fried chicken is rather cold now."

"Oh-h-h...dear...look, before you write me off as a complete jerk, please consider some mitigating factors. The flood...wrapping up school...and Sid Burk's body turning up in my uncle's barn. It's been crazy."

"Okay...I know you've had some problems." Lisa's voice became more sympathetic. "It's true that you didn't promise that you'd be here for lunch. But I was wondering why the phone didn't ring...and then when I got word you were last seen entering the sheriff's office..."

"I appreciate your concern. The inquest is over, and my aunt needs some groceries, but we've got a lot to talk about. What about tonight? Could you come over right after dinner?"

"Yes. I'd like to talk to you."

"Thanks for calling, Lisa."

As the remainder of the afternoon passed, Tim went through the motions of assisting his uncle and aunt with some chores, but his mind kept drifting to Lisa.

The Flinn farm was about a mile from the Whinney house. Shortly after helping his uncle and aunt move their belongings from Indiana to Ohio two summers ago, Tim heard that an attractive young lady lived in the vicinity. He tried to stumble across her path, and eventually learned from her that she had nursed similar desires.

It finally happened at the local feed store. They met, they talked, they felt a certain electricity that no law of accounting ever adequately explained. In any event, Tim started dating Lisa. It was her junior year of college, and she was majoring in accounting.

"Just how serious *is* this romance?" Martin had asked in one of his letters. Tim had no certain answer. He liked her. Some days he thought maybe yes, and other days he was uncertain. The bottom line was that his future would not always be in Ohio, and Lisa had spent a lifetime here. Tim assumed that he would leave OU before long in order to get a jump in salary and associate professor. Was there any sense in cultivating a relationship that would have to end? The more he gave in to the touch of those tender fingers, the more he might be setting the stage for a bitter farewell. So, what approach should he follow?

Before tackling his own question that evening, he served lime sherbet with fresh pineapple spears to his guest and himself.

"I hope I didn't sound like a shrew this afternoon. I was really worried about you."

He smiled at her. "Lisa, you'll have to wait until you're a minimum of eighty-five years of age before you'll have the least chance of sounding like a shrew."

"You deserve high marks for flattery. Now why don't you tell me what happened at this inquest?"

Tim repeated the experience, not failing to notice that her ash brown hair was as gorgeous as dark mahogany, her sparkling green eyes were as dazzling as emeralds, and the mouth and teeth were perfect. Utterly perfect. Beyond that, she seemed genuinely concerned about helping him defend his relatives.

"...and so, in summary, I think you can see the hurdles we face, and you may want to give some thought to...uh...leaving Ohio."

"Doing *what*?"

Tim slapped his forehead. "Nothing, nothing...I just misspoke myself."

Lisa nibbled a pineapple spear. "Can you think of any other explanation for those tire tracks by the older barn? I mean...could the killer have walked overland from Route 7 and used a cart or wagon to make the tracks?"

"My understanding is that the sheriff looked into that carefully. He found one or two old wagons in the area, but they were the wrong size, parked and loaded down with rusty junk, and so forth. They combed the area and considered all kinds of possibilities, but in the end only the eight people and their seven vehicles make any sense. Excluding my uncle and aunt, we have six vehicles and six suspects."

"Could there have been a car that got pushed into the river?"

"That's very similar to my four-wheel-drive, down-from-Route-7 theory. The problem is, all of this rain produced soft, mushy ground. You could make it over the pastureland from Route 7 and back, in a Jeep or something like that, but you'd leave horrendous ruts in the mud. There weren't any. Likewise, a car pushed down the embankment would leave tracks. They found none."

"Hmmm. So more and more, it looks as if one of the six moved the body."

"Yes. Conceivably the killer could've come in on foot, but a car had to be used to move the body to our barn, and leave the tracks there. That's why the sheriff keeps pressing the idea of someone's car being briefly stolen and then returned. Once again, everyone is saying 'Forget it, my car wasn't touched.'"

"But the killer might be wise to suddenly discover that his car *was* tampered with. Then there would be no limit to the list of suspects."

"True, but Sheriff Kruger is no dummy, and he realized early on that the cars were critical to his theory. So he asked people if their cars could've been used, and he inspected back seats and trunks for blood, water and mud. Nothing. The only answer is that the real killer had the time and means to be sure his or her car trunk bore no indication of the crime."

"I see. If you steal someone's car, and want to get it back before they find it's missing, you don't take the time to clean out the trunk."

"Yes. And if it's your own trunk, you *do* clean it carefully, because you don't want to answer any embarrassing questions about bloodstains."

Lisa swallowed another spoonful of sherbet. "Do you need an associate investigator?"

"Yes I do. Martin is coming on the thirty-first, and he...have you ever met Martin?"

"No. I suppose he's a licensed private detective, in addition to his other talents."

"Not exactly. He's an accountant. He and I...well, I guess I never told you, but during our senior year of college, we had to do some sleuthing. Drug smuggling, and unfortunately some of our close friends were involved. We made a big dent in the drug flow, and Martin and I gained some experience."

"He's the one you might be an accounting partner with someday?"

"Yes. We've talked about an accounting business, but as I started to say, he and I have matters to discuss. I really don't know his plans."

"And what about *your* plans?"

"I'll stay here until this mess is settled. I can't desert my uncle and aunt at a time like this."

"That makes good sense, Tim."

He gazed out the window. "I'm going to ask Martin to stay here a while. You could help, Lisa. For one thing, you could reassure him that Greenharbor is a delightful place to visit. And, I'd really like to have your help in proving my uncle and aunt innocent."

Lisa put her hands on Tim's and raised her eyes to meet his.

"You've got it."

* * *

Tim and Lisa found they were in complete agreement on the wisdom of questioning the out-of-town suspect before he returned to his home. Tim had already learned that Walter Rankin was staying at the Greenharbor Motel, and it proved an easy task to secure a Sunday afternoon appointment with him.

"Heard about the toolbox," were his first words of greeting as he flung open his motel room door to admit his two visitors. "Clumsy mistake by whoever killed Burk. Plain as day that someone wants to frame your uncle. But they've overdone it and established his innocence. Bunglers. Would you folks care for soda?"

"Yes, thanks. Have you met Lisa?"

"No...I don't think so."

"I'm Lisa Flinn."

"Pleased to meet you. I'll step out for that soda and be right back."

When they were alone in the room, Tim whispered to Lisa, "We want to get as much information as we can without making it sound as if we suspect him of murder."

"If the first gust was any indication, you may not need to ask any questions at all."

Tim watched observantly as Walter Rankin headed back to them, three bottles of Pepsi in hand. Rankin was tall and slim with broad shoulders, and a purposeful gait in his walk. His age was hard to guess, and Tim had not seen it in the sheriff's notes. The younger man surmised his host's age as past fifty, but probably not sixty.

"I'm from Cincinnati, you know," Mr. Rankin

divulged as he handed out elegant drinking glasses and dark blue coasters. "Thought this would be a boring trip. Even brought along some books to read. But no such thing." Rankin sipped some cola, as did the others.
"I understand you've had a visit from Deputy Nagle."
"Yes, he was here earlier. That man would make a good diplomat---if we had a national commitment to start wars."
"I take it that you've heard the evidence that points in my uncle's direction."
"Yes, and I tried to enlighten Nagle that his chief suspect is the one least likely to have committed the crime. Seriously now--what kind of a nitwit would it take to kill someone, drag the body to your own barn, leave your tools in the victim's house, and report everything to the sheriff? Nonsense! In what little I've spoken to your uncle and aunt, Tim, it's clear that they had no part in Burk's death."
"I agree totally. But can you see how the newest family comes under suspicion? Between Nagle harping on the negatives and someone planting evidence against Uncle Everett, we're hardly out of the woods."
"I've gleaned as much, and your own investigation has brought you here. Well sir, I hope you'll be pleased to hear that I'm going to hang around for a few days and look into the matter myself."
"That's very...uh...uh...constructive. Perhaps we can share information."
"Certainly. It's early to lock in to pet theories. But I'll hazard the opinion that the theater woman seemed a little defensive."
They talked for a few more minutes, without drawing up any specific plans to discover the murderer's identity. Then Tim and Lisa departed.
"What did you make of all that?" she asked as they rode northeastward out of Greenharbor.
"Hard to say. I'd like to sleep on it. Won't we have a chance to talk at the Memorial Day picnic tomorrow?"
"Yes, we will. Tim, don't forget that I start summer school in several weeks. That'll take me to Marietta at least four and a half days out of seven."
"If I can add Martin's assistance to yours, I think I'll have plenty of help."
"Don't forget that Mr. Rankin will be investigating also," Lisa said.
"Yes. Perhaps each of the eight suspects should conduct a personal investigation. Then the sheriff will have a novel-length report waiting for him at the end of

June."

"Highlighted by eight different conclusions as to the murderer's identity."

"Nothing is impossible," Tim laughed. "What courses are you taking this summer?"

"A basic income tax course and a governmental accounting course. I'm really going to need your help on the government course. The instructor normally requires a term paper."

"No problem. Just remember that Current Assets = Current Liabilities + Fund Balance. A fund balance represents the available spendable resources of the fund, unless there are certain restrictions, called reserves, to the fund balance."

"Oh, I'm sure it's more complicated than that simple formula."

"Well your course selection is fine. Government accounting and taxation are just two sides of the same coin: collecting and spending."

He drove her home and promised to see her again the next morning. Not having slept well on Friday or Saturday night, he was dead tired. Even his efforts to work on a research paper were punctuated with yawns and drooping eyelids.

At nine p.m. Tim gave up the struggle, took a shower, and wrapped a towel around his waist as he trudged off to his bedroom. Looking in the full-length mirror on the back of his door, he saw a slender, delicate-looking man with a mane of damp, curly brown hair. The bed looked inviting. He didn't even bother to locate a pair of undershorts, in which he usually slept. Putting the towel across his chair and turning off the light, he climbed naked into bed.

His last thought before dozing off was about Martin's visit. Would he stay? Would he help? Could they agree on an accounting practice in Athens? Nothing seemed more important than Martin's resourcefulness added to Tim's.

He slept soundly for five hours. Then, the yellow glow of a candle told him that the dream was starting anew.

No, he thought, tossing in bed and arguing with himself as a hapless patron might argue with a dictatorial projectionist. Not the search, the strange fruit, the ominous mountain, the black crows, all headed for the same ugly conclusion. No, not again...

Once more, the man with the changing face answered Tim's question. "My name is Midnight." He raised the gun. "Midnight means death." But for once, Tim jumped, frantically trying to avoid the deadly bullets.

Landing several feet to the side, he hoped the absence of pain in his body meant a reprieve from almost certain death.

But, to his horror, he realized that his colleague was still with him. When Tim had jerked his way out of the path of the gunfire, the bullets struck the figure behind him. A white shirt began to redden. The dark hair oozed blood and brain tissue. A once-handsome face was barely intact as four inches of flesh curled to the side.

As Tim screamed, Martin Zippa fell dead to the ground.

Chapter Five

The strongest objections to including depreciation would probably come from internal users, such as municipal finance officers, since many cities do not compile such information. However, this is not a compelling reason to exclude it.
Janet D. Daniels
Craig E. Daniels

As far as Tim was concerned, he had been mature and stoic long enough. He was disgusted and upset by his vibrant dream, and he was fully determined to get some sympathy.

"I hate it. I hate having a dream that I can't turn off," he said as he looked up at Lisa's sympathetic face. They had left the picnic crowd a quarter of a mile behind them, and hiked to a secluded clearing on King's Hill, on the north edge of Greenharbor. East of them was a view of the Ohio, which was now contracting by the day. Tim was lying on a blanket, and had his head cradled in Lisa's lap.

"Now I know you don't want me to recommend professional help," she said in a half-serious, half-chiding voice.

"I guess that's what I had in mind when I talked to O'Malley. For all the good it did." He smiled at her. "I was going to tell Martin about the dream...but is that wise? Maybe he'll find it a bad omen."

"Maybe you shouldn't tell him at first."

"Perhaps not." He closed his eyes. "It's very peaceful here. I wish it could be this peaceful all summer, but I somehow doubt it."

"Take each day as it comes."

"I've got something for you. A gift." He reached into his right front pocket and extracted a plastic bus token, red on one side and blue on the reverse. "This is yours."

She took it. "What on earth do I need this for?"

"It's symbolic. It's a hint of things that might happen. My way of saying...stick with me and you'll go places."

"Yeah...a circle around the campus on a bus. Big deal." She dropped the token into her pocket.

Tim moved to a sitting position. "As often as we come here, it might be appropriate to carve our initials into that mammoth oak tree at the edge of the clearing."

"There could be a pinch of sentimental value in that."

Tim stood up. "Of course, devoted naturalist that I am, I would never dream of cutting a tree."

"Oaks have been known to endure such minor scratches and survive."

When he made no effort to follow through on an inscription, Lisa took a tube of lipstick and scribbled both sets of initials on the oak that dominated the clearing.

"Remember the words of the philosopher, Lisa: time washes away all lipstick."

* * *

Tim survived Monday night without a recurrence of the bothersome dream. On Tuesday morning he rode with Vince Corbett to Ohio University, to give his last exam of the semester. As he waited somewhat impatiently for all the test forms to be turned in, he skimmed the *Post*, the student newspaper; then he absentmindedly scanned the last question on his exam.

33. How much of the gross domestic product represents government expenditures?
  A. 25%
  B. 35%
  C. 40%
  D. 45%
  E. None of above

The correct answer was C. Government entities are economically important.

* * *

After submitting his grades he returned to the farm in his adequately repaired Olds Cutlass. Tim made it through Tuesday with no word from Martin and no nightmare to jar his slumber. Wednesday morning was a logical time to interview the sixth suspect, Attorney Elston Grant, but the lawyer was still enmeshed in a courtroom trial in Cleveland.

Not willing to give up easily, Tim next drove to the Greenharbor Little Theater, to chat with Novia Dixon. But she was on a short vacation.

"I'm nothing if not persistent," Tim reassured himself as he tried the county law enforcement building for an update from the sheriff. But Kruger was attending a meeting out of town.

"Forget it," Tim said this time, and drove back to the farm. He arrived at the farmhouse just in time for a porkchop lunch.

Finally at five p.m., the big event came to pass. A

smile etched across Tim's face as a dark blue Chrysler convertible rolled to a stop in the Whinney driveway. A bumper sticker on the back proclaimed: "Happiness is positive cash flow."

"It's about time." Tim clapped Martin's shoulder, then made himself useful by carting two suitcases to the guest room.

"We'll get you settled in," Aunt Mildred promised as she supervised the unpacking. "Everett, why don't you put that in the closet for now? Martin, would you like something to drink? Tea? Lemonade? I'm sure you know that the only alcohol around here is in the liniment bottle."

Martin smiled. "Lemonade would be great."

"And you, Tim?"

"I'll have a double liniment and soda."

As Martin stretched out his tall, lean body in the living room's overstuffed chair and sipped his drink, Tim took a few moments to see if his friend looked any different. They had not seen each other in nine months.

Martin looked the same. The coal-black hair, the beige skin already sporting a deep summer bronze, and the perfect white teeth. Fate had made him a very handsome man.

"Your last letter said your neighbor's murder was unsolved," Martin interjected, true to form in his tendency to cut to the heart of any problem. "Is that still where it stands?"

"Yes, and by the way," Aunt Mildred frowned, "I heard today that our good friend Deputy Nagle has been asking a lot of nosy questions."

"Hostile fire will be returned," Tim commented. "Martin, while my aunt prepares supper, perhaps you and I could take a walk and discuss things."

"Sure, Tim. I'd like that."

It was a tranquil evening as the two friends ambled past the red barn and headed southward toward the gray haybarn. "I'll show you exactly where the body was found. But, you know, Martin, all of this is rather meaningless if you're going to leave in a few days, and stay invisible for two or three years. What about our old plan to open an accounting practice? Could we have one in Athens?"

"You never change, Tim. You want that practice, and you want *me* there, too."

"Well, not if I have to drag you into it. It'll only work if we're both happy with it."

Martin stopped walking. "I want it, Tim. I've made up my mind."

"But...your family...your firm? Surely they're

31

expecting you back."

Martin shrugged and managed a philosophical smile. "Families are nice, aren't they? Even though you're born into them, and generally can't do much to change them. And jobs can be about the same. Don't worry, Tim, I've prepared them for my departure."

"There's nothing I've wanted to hear more than that," Tim said with a smile.

They reached the older barn, and Tim pointed out where Sid Burk's body had been found. "Had he been shot here, there would've been much more blood."

"Any word on where he *was* shot?"

"That's one more item on the agenda when we meet with Sheriff Kruger."

"My car is at our disposal."

"Oh yes...that nifty car of yours. I don't suppose that was purchased with any of our 'drug money,' as you so loosely termed it?"

"Of course not. That money is in a separate fund, and I won't spend a penny of it without your agreement."

"Well, this summer could be the time we make the first withdrawal." Tim sat down on a bale of hay. "I still wonder about our decision on that money. Do you think we did the right thing?"

"You ask me that question once every six months, like clockwork. Yes Tim, we did the right thing. Our foolish college friends made the money, and the only thing we knew about it, when we finally uncovered their involvement, was that some of the bills were coded. They fled for their freedom, the cash was left in our hands, and what else could we have done?"

"Turn it in?"

Martin sighed. "We've been over this too many times. We'd already decided not to give evidence against our friends and hurt their families. Turning in that money might have proven their guilt---or raised questions about ours. And money held for evidence in that county had an odd way of evaporating. I held it, I laundered it, and now I've doubled it. So quit fretting. We've followed the most practical and the most moral course that was open."

"Okay. All right. But please quit calling it "drug money" and discussing it in print. Let's pretend it was a birthday gift from my uncle in Indiana. Remember, you are an ethical Certified Public Accountant."

"Fourteen thousand dollars. Not a bad gift."

"At today's prices we could blow it in a day. If we were stupid. Which we aren't."

"Agreed."

"Listen, there's one other thing you should know

before we start clearing up this unpleasantness hanging over my uncle and aunt."

"Which is?"

"I've been having a really weird dream. Seven nights in a row I've had the same dream, and the ending never changes---I get killed."

"Tim, Tim...you're becoming a hypochondriac. Always creating problems out of thin air, and then complaining until someone solves them for you."

"Martin, this is not an ordinary dream. It's very disturbing."

"But it's still a dream, isn't it? And not reality?"

"Well...yes...you're right."

"Then ignore it."

They returned to the farmhouse and enjoyed a savory fried chicken dinner.

"You know," Martin commented shortly after he finished a dishful of Aunt Mildred's cinnamon rice pudding, "what I'm looking forward to, after a year of the Chicago fast track, is the leisurely pace of some country living."

"So you have doubts that there'll be much excitement around Greenharbor?" Tim asked.

"I wouldn't think so."

Just then the phone rang.

"A case in point," Martin continued as he motioned toward the telephone, which was out of sight in the hallway. "That will probably be the feed store with a new order of seed, or an opportunity to buy some chickens."

"You've almost convinced me not to answer it." Tim disappeared into the dimness of the hallway and spoke with the caller for about two minutes.

When he returned to the living room where his uncle, aunt and guest were seated, he asked, "Martin, did we have any money riding on how electrifying that call would or wouldn't be?"

"Not even a penny."

"I was afraid of that." Tim paused a moment for effect, then relayed the caller's message. "That was Douglas Grant, our neighbor up the road. His life has been threatened, and he wants our help."

Chapter Six

First, government, particularly the federal government, performs the income/wealth redistributive function in society. Second, government specializes in producing public goods. It acts when the market fails--when firms lack the incentives to produce and consumers lack the incentive to pay for certain goods due to their nonappropriability.
                                            James L. Chan

Assuring his uncle and aunt that they could be of best use by staying near the phone, Tim joined his friend inside the Chrysler convertible for a quick ride northward on the old loop road to the Grant household.

"By the way," Martin asked as he watched for the second driveway on the left, "if we're going to be pursuing dangerous killers armed with .38s who like to put bullets through the heads of their victims, do we have any weapons of our own?"

"Well, my uncle owns a .22 rifle and a pelletgun to chase away stray dogs. But, I'm told the local authorities frown on private citizens carrying handguns. Don't investigative accountants use only balance sheets and income statements to solve crimes?"

"Perhaps they do, but if I'm going up against a .38 with your uncle's pelletgun, I would tend to feel I'm at a serious disadvantage."

"Things may not get that drastic. I'm very much a nonviolent person, and I plan to do all I can to avoid gunplay. There's his driveway."

Tim had never before been inside the luxurious house owned by Elston Grant. Aunt Mildred, who had managed to acquire plenty of information about the neighbors, once related that Grant was divorced and had lived alone until his nephew, Douglas, moved in.

It was young Douglas Grant who stood in the doorway and shook hands with first Tim and then Martin. The twenty-six-year-old paralegal, not quite as tall as his guests, seemed nervous and tired.

"Martin will be giving me a hand with my own investigation, as I mentioned on the phone."

"I understand. You're lucky to have someone able to help you on short notice, Tim...if it's all right to call you Tim."

"Please do. I wouldn't be comfortable with anything else."

"Same here," Martin interjected. "Call me Martin or don't call me at all."

Douglas smiled, but he was obviously not at ease. "Please follow me to the living room. May I fix either of you a drink?"

"Maybe later. I'd like to see this note you received, and discuss what if anything we can do to help."

The three of them took seats in the regally apportioned living room. "Just to have you here makes me feel better. Believe me, Tim, I've never been afraid to stay by myself. But now, with a killer on the loose, and a threat directed at me, it's...harder to be comfortable alone."

"Your uncle is still out of town, then?"

"Yes. He called yesterday and thought he would be tied up until Saturday."

"Very well, then, let's start at the beginning. You said on the phone that you came home from the office about six p.m."

"Yes...in a good mood, and having almost forgotten Sid Burk's death. I mean, I hadn't allowed it to bother me or to disturb me. Then, when I came to the front door, a note was stuck there." Douglas opened a drawer in the coffee table and handed a piece of white folded paper to Tim. Martin left his chair and stood behind his friend, enabling them to read the typed message at the same time.

SID BURK'S DEATH WAS NO ACCIDENT. NEITHER WILL YOURS BE. TRY TO AVOID DARK, LONELY PLACES. WHEN YOU THINK YOU'RE ALONE, YOU WON'T BE. IT IS YOUR FATE TO SUFFER A MOST TRAGIC DEATH.

"Have you shown this to the police, Mr. Grant?" Tim said finally.

"Please call me Doug...or Douglas. I realize we've had little opportunity to be friends, but...the way things are, we need to pull together. Anyway, some deputy answered, and suggested I bring the note in. But he said they would need to have a name, or someone stalking the house, before they could take action."

"That must have been reassuring," Martin said.

"You've put your finger on it...Martin. The note was bad enough, but the realization that some killer was free to do his work, while the sheriff waited for names...I...I lost my rationality for a few minutes.

"Then I remembered that right after the inquest, someone mentioned that you had plans to investigate, and the sheriff didn't object. I thought...well, maybe I needed the services of a private investigator. Someone nearby, that I could trust. I mean, we Grants are not as rich as people think, but there's some money available. Last week I cashed in a savings certificate for a thousand dollars. I'd like for you to take the money, Tim, and do some investigating on my behalf. The more effort we can muster to look for this killer, the better."

"Don't spend your money too quickly," Tim cautioned. "I'm not a licensed private investigator, so you couldn't pay me for that. I suppose I could legally be compensated for doing research on community problems, or something like that, as long as no one was raising any legal objection. Martin and I both are interested in governmental forensic accounting. You should keep in mind three other points before deciding to pay me anything. First, Martin, who is a CPA, will be my associate, and we'll both get some help from Lisa Flinn. Second, I subscribe to the sheriff's theory that there are only eight possible suspects...and, unless this note is a prank, whoever wrote it is Sid Burk's killer. Third, two of the eight happen to be my uncle and my aunt. I've spent two or three weeks with them almost every summer of my life, I've been with them through good times and heartaches, I've prayed with them in church, and I'm here to tell you that they are not murderers."

"Of course not," Douglas responded sympathetically. "In fact, it's hard to think that any of the eight people named by the sheriff could have any possible involvement with serious crimes."

Martin added, "We're going to keep digging until we discover who actually has some dangerous secrets."

"Yes, I understand. In fact, I gather that both of you have some free time. But as for me, the work schedule between my uncle's office and the law firm I work for in Woodsfield is very heavy. Please accept a down payment, Tim, and consider me a client...uh, research client or whatever you prefer."

"All right...Martin and I will do our best. Are you looking for some sleep-in security tonight?"

Douglas Grant produced another brief smile. "Thank you, but I couldn't impose. I have friends in Greenharbor with very secure locks on their doors, so I'm driving into town. I'll be fine. But please start your efforts right away. I'll meet with you sometime this weekend."

"That sounds good," said Tim. "Do you do any work with governmental units?"

"A little; mostly in fiduciary funds -- pensions, endowments, and agency funds."

"Great."

Tim knew that there are four types of fiduciary funds: Pension Trust, Nonexpendable Trust, Expendable Trust, and Agency Funds. The accounting procedures are different for each type. Pension and Nonexpendable Trust Funds use a commercial model, with full accrual, revenues recognized when earned, and expenses. Expendable Trust Funds use a governmental model, with modified accrual, revenues recognized when measurable and available, and expenditures. Agency Funds have no operations, since they do not record revenues and costs and no equity position. "Do you get involved with any accounting work?"

"Well, actually, I know very little about the accounting aspects."

"If you ever need any help," Tim said, "give me a call. I would be glad to help you."

Douglas then gave Tim a check for two hundred dollars, and packed a small suitcase.

"Shall we follow you into Greenharbor?"

"No... there's no need. I feel safe on the road."

The three of them left the house together, locking it behind them. Tim felt sure that Douglas Grant was unlikely to stay there alone at night until the murderer was captured.

After Doug's Mercury disappeared from view, Martin asked, "Is there anything else we can do here?"

"I'd be afraid of setting off an alarm. Let's get some sleep and start questioning suspects tomorrow."

"At least the field is narrowing. Surely Doug's uncle wouldn't be trying to kill him. So we're down to four suspects."

"Perhaps." Tim swung into the passenger's seat. "But first things first. Let's establish a motive. If it's anything like the drug case we handled, we might find that the carrot-and-stick monster of huge profits and minimal expenses on one side and lengthy prison terms on the other can turn very respectable people into very dangerous people."

"Agreed." Martin started the engine. "Wait a minute! We didn't even bring that note with us."

Tim waved the piece of paper in question. "I never leave a death threat behind."

Back at the Whinney house, Tim gave a brief explanation of Douglas Grant's predicament to Uncle Everett and Aunt Mildred. Then he showed Martin to the guest room, located next to his own room, and wrapped up his day with a shower.

With his robe on, Tim exited the bathroom and headed for bed. It was only ten o'clock, but he was exhausted and wanted a good night's rest.

It was approaching two in the morning when Tim's sleep was disturbed by the flicker of a yellow candle. Again he was searching for a man named Midnight. As always, the trail led to the awesome mountain, the five crows, the inescapable question, the deadly gun.

"No! No! No! Go away..." Tim was trying to struggle, then realized someone was holding his arms to his side.

"If you'll quit swinging, I'll turn the lamp on."

"Oh...okay." Tim felt sweat all over his body. He wondered how many people he had awakened.

The light clicked on and there was Martin, wearing nothing but a low-cut pair of dark blue briefs. He looked at Tim very thoughtfully. "The same dream you've had each time before?"

"Yeah."

"Maybe I'd better hear it."

Just then Aunt Mildred's voice echoed down the hallway. "Tim? What's the problem?"

Martin glanced downward. "I'm...not exactly well-dressed for a visit from your aunt."

"I'll take care of it." Tim bounded out of bed, revealing his own low-cut, dark brown briefs. He pulled on the robe and stepped outside his door.

"Sorry to be so noisy, Aunt Mildred." Tim shielded his eyes from the hall light she had clicked on. "I...uh...was headed for the bathroom and stubbed my toe."

"Are you sure you're okay? I thought somebody was being murdered."

"I'm fine. A bandage did the trick. Thanks for the concern, and I'll see you in the morning."

Aunt Mildred headed back to the bedroom she shared with Uncle Everett. "Hmmph. Enough racket to raise the dead..."

Tim slipped back into his room and peeled off the robe. "Don't look at me so harshly. I told you it was a nasty experience. You wouldn't listen."

"You're right, and I'm sorry. But Tim, we shared a room for two years and you never had dreams like that. Never."

Martin sat on the foot of Tim's bed and folded his bare legs beneath him. "Sit down, fellah. I want to hear every detail of this hellacious dream. Everything in it. Start talking."

Chapter Seven

Fraud cannot be eliminated, but if it is to be reduced and brought under control, management and internal auditors must forge a partnership to attack the problem. The strategy of this partnership should be to rely on both preventive measures and methods of detection.

Glenn E. Deck

Tim sat down in the straight-backed chair that faced the bed. "I wanted to tell you about the dream earlier. But when I tried to say that it had really bothered me, you dismissed it. You didn't want to hear it."

"I had our accounting business and my future move to Athens on my mind. Sorry if I seemed unsympathetic. Now...about this dream...if you could start at the beginning."

"Okay, here goes. It's a dream that divides itself into three parts. Each part is dominated by a color and a symbol, and each section conveys a little story. It's a very graphic visualization, and it's more than a fantasy. Somehow, it intuitively registers that it has meaning for the future."

"The dream always starts with a candle glowing. A yellow haze of candlelight dominates the opening. I see myself in a chair, maybe stretched out the way I am now, and I'm hearing words. As if a radio newscast were on. A voice starts talking about a search for Midnight. It seems that he's a mysterious man who has disappeared. The last thing the voice says is that people everywhere are looking for him. Then I see three candles, and I begin to think about locating this man myself.

"The second segment is dominated by a large bed of roses, covering a hillside. The roses are a deep red, almost too red, and that color is the controlling tint of this part of the dream. I find myself at a kind of monastery, and I seek some advice from a monk. His clothes are maroon, and before answering my questions, he urges me to have a piece of fruit. The fruit he serves me is white---very, very white. At first I'm afraid of it, but then I tell myself that apples are white, and I eat it."

"And it poisons you."

"No, it's delicious."

"I'm sorry. Keep going."

"I'm there because I've started to develop an almost idealistic feeling that I'm the best qualified person to find the missing man. But the monk pours cold water on my wishes, figuratively speaking. He says I'm too young, too inexperienced, sure to fail, etc. Reluctantly I come to agree with him, and leave. As I walk away, I see three more red roses, growing separately along the road."

"The third segment is louder and more graphic. It starts with the pealing of bells, and I notice that the three large bells I hear are black---jet black. Two things have happened since my visit with the monk. First, I've gathered my courage and decided to go looking for the man named Midnight. Second, I've enlisted your help. Together, we follow the clues we find to the base of a huge, ominous mountain. A pale green moss seems to cover the entire mountain, but the image of those black bells remains central to my thoughts as we start climbing ahead. When you take a breather, I surge past you, and it's then that I notice five black crows flying overhead."

"Trudging on ahead, and for some odd reason not paying much attention to you, I come around a bend in the trail and find a tall, slim man in a pale green overcoat. His face is both strange and familiar. I tell him, 'I've seen you before, but I don't know you. Who are you?' He replies, 'My name is Midnight.' Now in every dream but one, I've frozen in my tracks and he mows me down. The next to last time I dreamed it, I jumped to one side, but you were murdered."

Martin responded softly, "I think I'll select ending C. Neither of the above is murdered."

"I truly wish that Morpheus or whoever supervises dreams would give me that option. As it is, I'm a paralyzed witness to my own death. I feel the bullets entering, the pain burning, blood and flesh exiting, and I see a pool of red blood swallowing my body...just before I wake up with my heart pounding."

"Hmmm...and you've dreamed it how many times?"

"Nine, Martin...that's nine too many."

"Strange. Very strange." Martin snapped his fingers. "Let's try hypnosis."

"I don't know anyone around here who practices hypnosis at a professional level."

"Then I'll find someone. We need to unravel this problem."

"Well...okay...but as for now..." Tim stood up and yawned.

"Okay, but I don't need any more jungle war cries while I'm in a strange room alone. Tell you what, Tim...I just happen to have my sleeping bag with me..."

Martin vanished into the guest room, then reappeared with a sleeping bag in one hand and a pair of pants in the other. "What you need is a kindhearted roomie who will muffle any further wails and screams by inserting a pillow in your mouth."

"Well...if you want to sleep in here...I guess it's a preventive measure of some merit."

"It's also a good idea." Martin crawled into the sleeping bag. "Now turn out the lamp and be quiet."

Tim settled back into his own bed, but he ventured one final thought before drifting off to sleep. "Martin, in doing what we're doing to help my uncle and aunt, has it occurred to you that we're already searching for a person named Midnight?"

★ ★ ★

After breakfast, Tim and Martin headed for the sheriff's office. "You realize," Martin said as the warm morning wind enveloped the open convertible and ruffled his hair, "I've never met the winsome young lady whose picture decorates the nightstand in your room."

"She'll be back from her summer school classes tomorrow afternoon."

Following Tim's directions, Martin parked his convertible across the street from the recently completed county law enforcement building. The young men had to wait only two minutes before being ushered into the sheriff's private office.

"Good morning, Tim. I understand your research is moving right along. And who might your young friend be?"

"This is Martin Zippa. Martin, Sheriff Don Kruger."

After a polite introductory handshake, Martin added on his own, "I've been a close friend of Tim's since high school, and I'll do everything I can to help him find the real killer of his uncle's neighbor."

"Then we're all sailing for the same port."

"That's right." Tim pulled out the threatening note addressed to Douglas Grant. "Have you heard about this message?"

The sheriff read the note, frowned and read it again. "Only vaguely, but I haven't gone over all my reports from yesterday. Fill me in."

Tim repeated what he knew. "I think Doug is genuinely frightened, and he surely has good reason to worry about his safety."

"I agree. But I also don't relish the expense of a twenty-four-hours-a-day guard at the Grant property. Any chance you folks out there could form something of a watch group?"

"Yes, I suppose so. The only problem is going to be

the confidence factor. Who's watching the person who's supposed to be watching me? Can one afford not to watch all the other watchers? You get my point---the only satisfying solution is to jail the killer."

"You're right. Mind if I photocopy this note?"

When the sheriff returned, Tim was ready with his list of questions. "You said you recovered the bullet from Burk's head. Is it in good enough shape to match it with one fired from the same gun?"

"Yes, I believe so. Can you find me the gun?"

"I'm trying. Is there any further word on Burk's exact location when he was shot?"

"We can't be certain, but we've found some well-scrubbed bloodstains on the concrete floor of his garage. We think he died there."

"What about the man himself? How did he earn a living?"

"Worked on and off at a gas station about ten miles north of Greenharbor. Did some farm work now and then. It appears he inherited a few dollars when his father died, eleven years ago. I guess he's been a careful spender."

"What about my suggestion that he might have been involved in something shady?"

"Hard to prove, Tim. The man only had one arrest, thirteen years ago when he was twenty-five. Seems he and a buddy were likely suspects in a break-in at that wood stove manufacturing place just south of Clarington. But the evidence against them was less than overwhelming, and the prosecutor dismissed it."

"That's not much, but I'd like to pursue it."

"Be my guest."

"What about drugs? Any hint that Burk was involved in drug sales?"

"No trace of any drugs in his body. No needle marks. No drugs in his house. I'd call it unlikely."

"Sheriff...do *you* have a theory as to why he was killed?"

"No. But this business about a threat to Douglas Grant adds a new dimension. It may supply some rhyme and reason to Burk's death, if we can put the right pieces together."

Martin leaned forward in his chair. "Did Sid Burk own the property he lived on?"

"Yes."

"Who gets it now? And who gets any money he might have left behind?"

The sheriff thumbed through several sheets of paper on his desk. "His only living relative appears to be his mother. Molly Burk is seventy-three and in poor health...living in a senior citizens' apartment complex north of here in Barnesville."

"Well, maybe *she* knows something."

"Maybe. If so, she wasn't disposed to tell Deputy Nagle about it."

Tim pocketed his small list. "That does it for me. I'm out of questions."

"Good luck, fellahs."

Tim and Martin took a leisurely drive around Greenharbor, and headed back to the farm.

"You can quit worrying that the sheriff is way ahead of you, Tim. It sounds as if you're both stuck in the same mudhole."

"We're overlooking something. There's a motive here...a solid reason for killing Burk...and we're not seeing it."

Shortly after lunch, Tim decided to interview Molly Burk before continuing his plan to question each of the six suspects. Barnesville being fairly small, it was not hard to locate the phone number for a senior citizens' complex there.

"I'm calling long distance from Greenharbor," Tim said as he held the receiver with his left hand and accepted a glass of lemonade from Martin with the other. "Can you give me the phone number for Mrs. Molly Burk?"

"I can," replied a subdued voice, "but no one's there. Perhaps you don't know...Mrs. Burk died yesterday."

"*Died*? Died of what?"

"A heart attack, I believe."

"Heart attack my foot! When are they doing the autopsy?"

"Why...why...I'm not sure there'll be one. She was old...and ill...and the cremation is set for two p.m. this afternoon."

Chapter Eight

Cities with strong financial viability and that participate in the Certificate of Conformance Program report more timely than do less financially sound, nonparticipating cities. Cities subject to state-mandated accounting regulation report more slowly than cities not subject to that regulation.
P.D. Dwyer
E.R. Wilson

A glance at his watch told Tim that it was one twenty. That gave him only forty minutes until Molly Burk's body, and whatever incriminating evidence it might still retain, would be lost forever. He tried a fast call to the sheriff's office in Belmont County, but the deputy who answered had little enthusiasm for intervening.

"We've got to go up there and stop that cremation," Tim told Martin. "The time factor is stacked against us. But we just might be able to get in there and stop them, when they would ignore a voice on the phone. Want to try it?"

"I'm ready."

"Great. Let's go."

They raced to the closest car. Tim leaped into the front passenger's seat and Martin's convertible took off. Had there been an expressway between Greenharbor and Barnesville, the rapidly dwindling minutes left would have been sufficient. But, the roads being what they were, Martin had to go south, then west, then north, including a trip through Woodsfield, just to reach the halfway point of their alacritous journey.

As the Chrysler arrowed past Somerton, Martin commented, "We're never going to be there by two o'clock."

"You're right," Tim said as he again consulted an Ohio roadmap.

"These roads are infuriating."

"That's true." Tim sighed, and attempted to fight off a growing sense of pessimism. "Sid Burk's possessions and property go to his mother. Now she's dead. We'd better find out who inherits next."

"Are you thinking that the inheritor will either be the next to be murdered, or will be the murderer himself?"

"I think that's *very* likely. However, if we have nothing but ashes to work with, it'll be hard to prove a double murder."

"Correct. I'll bet killers throughout the country

just love cremation."

It was past two o'clock when they reached the town of Barnesville. With surprisingly little difficulty they found the funeral home that housed the crematory. A memorial service for Molly Burk had been held that morning, and the only two people witnessing the cremation were the funeral home director and his assistant.

As Tim rushed into the large room that contained the crematory, he decided that there was nothing to lose by trying a little dramatic pushiness.

"I demand that this cremation be stopped!" he shouted as he sprinted to a halt in front of the funeral home director.

The middle-aged man did not seem impressed. "In that case, I hope you brought your magic wand and plenty of ice."

Martin had remained calm. "In other words, it's too late to reverse the process?"

"Exactly. Once you fire this baby up and put the remains inside, there's no stopping anything. You're talking 3,000 degrees and disintegration of all tissues." Tim stared blankly at the metallic, box-shaped structure before him. It looked very much like a home furnace, but longer and more enclosed. The funeral home director was not one to abandon his routine without good reason. "If you'll stand back, gentlemen, we have to break up the bone."

The assistant rolled the sliding doors apart, and the director picked up a poker-like rake. "Without some pulverization there's too much bone left intact," he explained as his gloved hand inserted the rake through an oblong opening in the middle of the heavy door that separated the living from the dead.

Through the window-like slot, Tim could see the last vestiges of a skeleton. A wave of furious heat swept toward him, as the clanking rake turned Molly Burk's skeleton into a grotesque pile of gray and white dust. A feeling of emptiness flooded his thoughts. The flesh, the organs, the fluids---the thousand and one complexities that made a human body distinct---could ever so easily be reduced to a pile of ash resembling what was left when one burned the morning trash. Somehow it sickened him.

"The coroner approved this?" Martin asked.

"Certainly. We don't lift a finger without a signed release."

"But there was no autopsy?"

"I understand there wasn't. I had met the lady once or twice, and she was definitely frail."

"We might as well go," Tim mumbled.
Before leaving Barnesville, they visited the complex where Molly Burk had lived, and chatted with two of her neighbors. The woman had not been in good health, but neither was she at death's doorstep. She had suffered previous heart problems. Also, there was no record kept of visitors at the complex. Virtually anyone could have dropped by, stated almost any plausible pretext, and offered a deadly item of food or drink. "It could've been a total stranger," Tim mused as he returned to the passenger's seat of their car. "He could've gagged her and injected her---left a nasty bruise on some part of her body---and where does all of our evidence go? Up in smoke."
"Agreed. I also agree that the coroner could've been more vigilant. From what I read, far too many deaths are excluded from the autopsy process. But merely having her body wouldn't guarantee finding the killer. He could've sneaked in her door, blasted her with his .38 and a silencer, then disappeared. That would've given us clues and carnage galore, but no guarantee of unmasking the killer."
"That's right. At present, he or she is making the moves, and the best we can do is respond to what happens. I accept that rationally, but you can bet that I don't accept it emotionally."
"Ditto. Shall we go back to Greenharbor?"
"Might as well."

* * *

Despite his disappointment, Tim found his appetite in time for supper, and finally succeeded in arranging an interview with Novia Dixon, the next person on his list of suspects.
"I think you'll like her," Tim explained as he and Martin prepared for a seven p.m. meeting at the theater director's home. "She's definitely show-biz---a little high-strung, full of vim, flashy in a polished sort of way."
"It's too bad we're not seeing her at a rehearsal. Then you could rush in and yell 'I demand that this play be stopped!'"
"I'm sure there are a few patrons of the Greenharbor Little Theater who would approve of such an edict, judging by some comments I've heard about recent performances. Anyway, we'd best get going."
Precisely at seven p.m. Novia Dixon opened the door of the small cottage she rented and ushered her two visitors inside. The tall, blonde woman looked younger

than her thirty-six years. "Something to drink?" she offered. "Iced tea? Orange soda? A Coke?"

"I could handle a Coke," Martin replied.

"And you, Dr. Whinney?"

"Nothing for me. And please call me Tim."

"Excellent. First names are nicer and friendlier. Please sit down while I pour."

Two minutes later, as Novia and Martin sipped their drinks, Tim said, "I would think that the financial frustrations of running a local theater group would prove burdensome and discouraging."

"It helps to have realistic expectations. I knew this wasn't New York City when I moved here, ten years ago."

"So by now you've come to think of Greenharbor as your home?"

"I guess you could say that. I have several good friends here---mostly female, unfortunately---and some relatives. I'm satisfied. Fame and fortune are two commodities I can live without."

Tim quietly cleared his throat. "You probably know that I'm doing some research on the death of Sid Burk."

"No I didn't, but that sounds like a good idea."

"Martin here will be assisting me."

"A very able-bodied assistant, by all indications."

"Novia, did you ever meet Sid Burk?"

"No, I don't think so. I'm sure he had nothing to do with the local theater. In fact, I look at my presence in the area where he died as totally circumstantial."

"Yes...that will probably prove true for five of the six main suspects. Tell me, on the evening you were there, did you speak with both Mrs. Barger and Mr. Sumoto?"

"Yes I did."

"Did either of them seem nervous---preoccupied---not totally themselves?"

"No, they both seemed fine. They were friendly, willing to chat...I'm sure none of us had any idea that Sid Burk was being murdered...or rather was murdered before I arrived."

"I see. Any questions, Martin?"

The black-haired young man took another sip from his drink and placed the glass on an end table. "You serve a tasty drink. I wanted to ask how well you know Douglas Grant."

"He...stops by to see a performance every now and then. Oh... about four years ago he did a very small part in one of our plays. He was good. I've asked him to try out on other occasions, but he always begs off because of his work schedule."

"Does he come alone or with someone?"

"He's almost always with a female friend. Since I've been here he's dated at least five or six girls...young women. They are invariably very nice and very pretty. To be honest about it, most of the single young men in this town are constantly dating someone. Pairing is quite the thing."

"Can you think of any reason why someone might want to harm Douglas Grant?" Martin continued in his soft, casual manner.

"Douglas? I've never heard anyone say a word against him. He's a very pleasant and well-liked young man."

"Yes..." Tim added with a touch of somberness. "We seem to be afloat in a town of pleasant, charming and nonviolent people. But somebody out there is less than pleasant beneath the phony exterior. That's why Sid Burk is dead, and why his mother is now dead."

"His mother?"

"Yes. She lived in Barnsville and died yesterday. We have reason to believe that the actual cause of death was poisoning."

"How awful!"

"Precisely. Perhaps the only way to get a handle on who's responsible for these crimes is for those of us who are innocent to stop seeing the best in everybody, and look for flaws, motives and a potential for violence. It's there, believe me."

"I do believe you. A successful theater director has to be a keen student of human behavior."

There was a brief silence, then Martin picked up the slack. "We might as well finish our who-knows-whom survey. You knew Verna Barger and Ling Sumoto. How about Elston Grant and this visiting businessman, Walter Rankin?"

"I met Mr. Rankin for the first time at the inquest. Naturally I know Elston Grant. He's a civic-minded attorney with a finger in a dozen pies. He's made some small contributions to the support of our theater group, but nothing like the generous amounts that Mr. Sumoto has given us."

Tim frowned, then slowly stood up. "That about does it. If you develop any fresh ideas about Sid Burk's death or potential enemies for Douglas Grant, please let me know."

All three of them stood, and Novia picked up both drinking glasses. "I will, Tim. I'd like to invite you and Martin to come and see our next play. We're doing *The Little Foxes*, starting June sixteenth."

"Ah!" Martin's face lit up. "One of my favorite plays."

"I'm sure you'll enjoy it."

"I'm certain of it." Martin took her hand and squeezed it gently rather than shaking it. "It's been nice meeting you."

"A pleasure. A true pleasure."

Tim thanked her again for her cooperation, then headed toward the front door. "We'll be on our way."

"If I hear anything, Dr. Whinney---Tim---I'll get in touch."

"I appreciate it. Good night."

Martin stepped to the open doorway, then turned toward Novia. "I'll stay in touch whether you have any clues or not."

She rested her arm on a small bookcase. "I'm sure we'll see each other again. Good night, Martin."

Returning her friendly smile, he stepped out into the night sky, gently closing the door.

Inside the convertible, Tim looked in Martin's direction and shrugged. "What else is there to ask, Martin? She has a very smooth and credible story that she knows nothing, and wants to be excused as a suspect. What else can we do---slap her around until she confesses?"

"A very nice lady. If you want to slap her around, then let *me* hold her."

"She might be a little old for you, Martin."

"Nope. She's under forty."

"Oh? What will your female age limit be when you're forty yourself?"

"Could be eighty. I'm getting more liberal every year."

"Well, that's fine, but..." Tim's attention was taken by someone he saw on the street. "There's Lyda. Hang tight a minute, Martin. I need to see this lady."

Tim left the convertible and crossed the street, walking toward a cheerful-looking, slightly plump black woman, Lyda Sparlin, who was an employee of the Flinn family. To Tim, she was more than that. In the nearly two years he had known her, he had recognized in Lyda a certain strength of character that impressed him. They had become friends.

Standing with Lyda was a tall, attractive black man whom Tim thought he recognized.

"Well, Tim! What a pleasant surprise. And I think you already know my cousin, Shawn."

"Of course." Tim extended his hand to Shawn. "I *thought* I recognized you. We graduated together from OSU."

"Right, right. Tim Whinney, the accounting ace."

"You find OSU grads everywhere," Tim said as he motioned for Martin to join them. "That's Martin Zippa in the convertible over there. He graduated with us."

"Oh yeah. I remember Martin."

They exchanged some small talk, and Shawn invited both Tim and Martin to visit Sparlin Farm.

"I've got the whole place to myself---and I'm real close to your uncle's farm. Come on over and we'll play some cards."

"Okay. I'll give you a ring first."

"Don't bother. No need, no phone."

"Oh, yes...you've been out of town for a while. New Orleans, did someone say?"

"Yeah. Playin' a little music. And when that gets slow, I make a buck or two as a carpenter."

"He's a bundle of talent," Lyda said as she clutched her cousin's arm.

"We'll all get together soon," Tim promised. "There've been some unusual happenings out on Old Nelson Road that we need to talk about."

* * *

Back at the farmhouse, Tim decided to try one or two phone calls before ending his efforts for the day. Earlier he had tried to set some wheels in motion, and he wanted to see if any of them were spinning. Knowing that Sheriff Kruger was working an evening shift, Tim tried that number.

"Sheriff? Tim. Anything yet on where the Burk money and property will go?"

"Yes, I've got two tidbits for you. First of all, neither Sid nor his mother left much of an estate. After his burial and her cremation, there won't be a thousand dollars left, according to her attorney. Hardly worth killing for."

"You're right. Was Sid Burk's property free of debt?"

"Yes it was. Because he died first, it passes from him to her to her heir. Here's the kicker. Only three or four days before her death, Molly sent her attorney an amendment to her will. It's witnessed, and he thinks it'll be valid. All real property--meaning Sid Burk's house and ground--will be inherited by one of our six suspects."

"Name please."

"Our number one attorney here in town, and still the only unquestioned suspect--Elston Grant."

Chapter Nine

Governmental accounting functions in an environment different from the private sector, and thus specialized accounting standards for state and local government are both justified and necessary.
                                    Walter L. Johnson

By Friday morning, Tim was chomping at the bit to question Elston Grant. However, a pre-breakfast phone call to his secretary in Greenharbor revealed no change in Mr. Grant's plan to conclude his legal work in Cleveland that evening, and be back in Greenharbor on Saturday morning.

"So," Martin asked between mouthfuls of cereal, "will there be a line of people waiting to bombard Grant with questions?"

"No, the sheriff is arranging a single interview session so that he, Nagle and I can get Grant's responses without a series of visits."

"That's helpful. Also, it could be my opportunity to meet this deputy that your aunt is so fond of."

"Nagle? To know him is to love him."

"You put infinitives to such sarcastic use, Tim. What's our first project today?"

"My plan is to interview all six of the murder suspects. So far I've talked to three of them. Today we'll visit the fourth person on my list, Ling Sumoto."

"I know him. He's one of the reasons I'm here. He's a client of my firm."

"Really? What are you doing for him?"

"He's on the city council and a member of the audit committee. He may hire me to audit Greenharbor."

"A small world," Tim said as he shook his head.

Martin offered to help Aunt Mildred with the breakfast dishes, but she wouldn't hear of it. The two investigators gathered what notes they had, and headed for Greenharbor.

Martin checked the rearview mirror and slipped on his aviator-style sunglasses as the Chrysler convertible with the personalized license plate CPA-1 pulled onto Ohio Route 7. "What are we trying to draw out of these interviewees? What results are we gearing our questions toward?"

Tim gave the subject a moment's reflection. "It's unlikely that we'll sweep the deck with any confessions or cover-blowing blunders from these folks. I'm tuning in to the aura, the ring...I guess the feel of what each one says. So if I miss some logical inconsistency in a

story, perhaps you'll catch it."
"I'll try."
They parked in front of a conservative, three-story office building and headed for Mr. Sumoto's business office on the first floor. His secretary, an attractive Oriental woman, escorted them into her employer's office. The tall, dignified man stood and smiled. "So good of you to come and see me, Dr. Whinney." He shook hands with them and invited them to have seats. "And this is the associate of whom you spoke?"
"Yes. This is Martin Zippa."
"So good to meet you." Mr. Sumoto looked confused. "Don't I know you?"
"Yes, Mr. Sumoto. I hope to audit Greenharbor this year. We spoke last week, and I'm to visit with you tomorrow with respect to the audit."
"Great."
"I'll be ready," Martin said.
The secretary rolled in a tray containing tea and sugar cookies. As usual, Martin did not need a second invitation. Tim declined at first, but finally decided to join the others in sipping a cup of tea.
Mr. Sumoto returned his cup to its saucer. "Martin Zippa sounds like an Italian name. And if you'll forgive me for saying it, you look Italian, Mr. Zippa."
"You're correct. Italian on both sides of the family tree."
"Italy is a vibrant, beautiful land. So rich in history. I've been there twice on business trips." The middle-aged traveler spoke softly, at times seeming to be lost in thought. "I suppose it was my fondness for Italy that led me to buy the Italian restaurant over on the south edge of the town square. Quite a mistake, really. I know little about restaurants and even less about the proper cooking of Italian food. So my wife began to operate it a number of years ago. A shame, really. That's how she met her boyfriend." Mr. Sumoto sipped some more tea and looked at Martin. "I don't suppose you know anything about restaurants?"
"My father and uncle manage one in Chicago. I've worked there."
"Is that so? My, my...how fortune can play strange tricks." He broke a cookie in two, easily and unobtrusively. "But...I am probably straying far away from the subject that is pressing on your heart." His eyes were now gazing steadily at Tim. "Do you have some questions for me about the recent murder, Dr. Whinney?"
"Yes. Highly predictable questions, I'm afraid. You probably know that my own investigation is aimed at clearing my uncle and aunt."

"Yes. I know."

"Two other developments are worth mentioning. After Sid Burk's death, his mother died under suspicious circumstances. Also, Douglas Grant received a written threat against his life."

"That is distressing news." His voice was mildly sympathetic, but his face showed no reaction.

"Mr. Sumoto, did you know Sid Burk at all?"

"I'm certain that we never spoke. But it's a small town...we could have passed on the street, or something like that. Running for political office, I might have met him."

"Have you had any thoughts as to why someone would want Sid Burk dead?"

"None."

"What was your final decision on Orick Farm---to buy or not to buy?"

"Not to buy." A wry smile crossed the man's face. "I was looking for a piece of property for a three-party exchange. Anyway, I have a buyer for one of my tracts of land, but I need to find some land that my buyer can purchase to trade me for my land. Do you understand?"

"Yes sir," Tim said. "I teach accounting at Ohio University. You don't wish to be taxed on the gain."

"Right. As you know, I have 45 days after I transfer my land to the buyer to identify some other real estate. Orick Farm proved to be less than a bargain."

"Is the third party one of the suspects?" Tim asked.

"No."

"Have you ever been a business partner with Elston Grant, the attorney?"

"No. We cross paths at council meetings of course. But we've never invested in a project together."

Tim finished his tea. "Martin, what else should we ask about?"

Martin glanced at a page of his notes. "Mr. Sumoto, who's the present owner of Orick Farm?"

The man started to answer, blinked, then slowly moved his hand to his chin. "You know, I'm not really certain. At first, I thought it was in the hands of the late Mrs. Orick's heirs. But Mrs. Barger strongly implied that the family had sold. She referred to a 'present owner' without giving me a name."

Tim reached over to the tray and picked up a sugar cookie. "In chatting with my aunt, who met Mrs. Orick last fall, I gathered that Mrs. Orick had sold the property, but retained the right to live there until her death."

"That could be."

"Well," Tim reflected, "a half-hour's research at the county courthouse should tell us who owns the place now."

"Yes." Mr. Sumoto gazed out his window for a few moments, then turned back to Tim. "Will you be spending the summer here, Professor Whinney?"

"Probably only part of it. And why don't you call me Tim? I'm more comfortable with that."

"Tim and his friend Martin," the black-haired accountant added.

Mr. Sumoto gave them a brief but courteous nod. "Perhaps the protagonist and deuteragonist, as the drama of these crimes unfolds." He glanced toward Martin. "So, Martin, I'll see you tomorrow at Grant's office?"

"Yes, I'll be there."

"We need help with the financial aspects of the city."

* * *

Because his afternoon plans did not afford him the necessary time to visit the county courthouse, Tim phoned in a request to Sheriff Kruger for the identity of the current owner of Orick Farm. That done, and their noon meal completed, Tim asked his house guest if he liked governmental accounting.

"It's rather exciting to be an investigative accountant. Some strange things can happen when one is looking for fraud."

"For example?" Tim asked. "Maybe you can help me give some real live examples in my lecture on fund accounting. It gets boring when I tell my students that expendable funds use the modified accrual basis, which employs the flow of current resources measurement focus. Modified accrual requires changes to accrual procedures to accommodate a liquidity perspective. The major changes relate to revenue recognition and the use of expenditures. Two criteria are used to determine revenue recognition: the revenue source must be measurable and available. Measurability means that the amount of revenue to recognize is known or can be reasonably estimated."

"I know what you mean. Be sure to tell them that expendable funds must use the flow of financial resources measurement focus and the accrual basis whenever the Governmental Accounting Standards Board allows implementation of Statement No. 11."

Martin thought for a moment. "So you need a war story. In January, this year, I was working on the records of a small town in southern Illinois. While auditing the permit fees, I noticed some discrepancies in cash collections. One of the city clerks had the duty of supervising cashiering operations and making a deposit of the permit fees at the end of each day. Over a three-year period there were no reconciliations of deposits to permits issued."

"The clerk's supervisor said that he trusted her. I found that the clerk would keep some of the cash collected for Thursday and Friday of each week. Over the three-year period she had embezzled more than $35,000. Eventually I discovered that the supervisor and clerk were having an affair, even though both were `happily married.'"

"Wow! A good story. What happened?"

"Since the clerk's husband was not reporting this income for tax purposes, he had to avoid a public trial. So he was quite willing to settle favorably with his wife."

* * *

The next person on Tim's list of suspects was Verna Barger, the real estate broker. But since she was out of town for the afternoon, Tim contented himself with leaving word at her office that he wanted to see her as soon as possible, hopefully the next morning.

At three p.m., Lisa Flinn called the Whinney number to announce her return from her first week of classes in Marietta.

"Why don't you drive on over here?" Tim asked her on the phone. "There's someone that I want you to meet."

Fifteen minutes later, Lisa rolled to a stop in the aging Ford station wagon that her parents kept as a second car. She stepped out of her vehicle and asked Tim, "Okay, where is he? I've been waiting a long time for this."

"He's inside, in the guest room that my aunt is beginning to refer to as Martin's room. I made the mistake of showing him the English grammar book that I brought back from College. He's been absorbed in it ever since."

"*An English grammar?*"

They walked into the house. "When you get to know Martin, you'll discover that he has an abiding passion for at least two things---airplanes and language studies. That's just how he is...it's an incurable condition."

"Mercy."

Tim and Lisa stepped into the guest room and found Martin thumbing through the grammar book. He looked up and smiled. "So I finally get to meet the girl in the picture. It's a lovely picture, but it hardly does you justice."

She returned his smile. "And I've waited a long time to meet you. Maybe this will be the start of a long-term friendship."

Tim folded his arms. "And now that you two have established an amicable *working* relationship, let's see if our three-person team can solve two murders."

Chapter Ten

If performed properly, a single audit yields benefits beyond compliance with a federal audit requirement. These benefits include accurate and timely financial statements that communicate results of operations to the public. In addition, the audit should provide suggestions for improvements in management systems, internal controls, and operating procedures.
          J.F. Morgalio
          Karen S. McKenzie

  On Saturday morning Tim and Martin walked into the law office of Elston Grant. Sheriff Kruger and Deputy Nagle were already seated. Looking relaxed as he sat behind a large oak desk was Elston Grant, forty-four. Soft-spoken and well-dressed, the lawyer lit his pipe and nodded as introductions were made.
  The first question came from Sheriff Kruger. "Mr. Grant, how well did you know Sid Burk?"
  "Not too well. We spoke only in passing."
  "Then you knew very little about his finances?"
  "Next to nothing."
  Deputy Nagle inserted a question. "Any idea who killed him?"
  "No. His death came as a shock and a surprise to me."
  "Mr. Grant," the sheriff continued, "would you care to explain why Molly Burk decided to will her property to you?"
  "I knew nothing about that until her attorney phoned me last night. I hardly knew the woman."
  "So out of the clear blue, she decided to will everything she owned to a total stranger."
  "It appears to be just that. However, I represent several charitable and public service organizations in Greenharbor. I can only surmise that Mrs. Burk associated my name with some public-spirited entity that I work with or work for, and decided to trust my good judgment."
  Sheriff Kruger tapped his pencil against his small notepad. "It gets stickier. Two years ago, Mrs. Orick sold her property, still called Orick Farm although it's hardly any bigger than your place. The arrangement allowed her to live there until her death. She died this past March, and an autopsy confirmed a natural death due to stroke. But the point is, she sold Orick Farm to Sid Burk. He owned his place and hers. Somebody killed Sid, and his elderly mother then owned

both places. Now she has died, and a last-minute change in her will puts all of her property in your lap. Now you're quite sure, Mr. Grant, that you know nothing about all of this?"

The attorney angled his pipe into an ashtray. "Not a thing. Other than a hello-nice-day-isn't-it, I didn't know Mrs. Orick or Sid Burk. I don't think I ever met Molly Burk. I never asked the Burk family for anything. They never called me and said they were fans of mine, and planned on giving me something. It's a conundrum to me. And I haven't seen this amended will of hers. Maybe there's another Elston Grant. A distant cousin? An old lover? Anybody check on that?"

Sheriff Kruger pulled a small piece of paper from his pocket. "Here's how it reads: 'I hereby bequeath all of my property and assets to Mr. Elston Grant, the attorney who works in Greenharbor, Ohio.' Now surely you don't know of another attorney with your name, working here in this small town, do you?"

"Certainly not. Guess I'll retreat to the theory that she was associating me with some charity."

Nagle cleared his throat. "You now own three pieces of property, all touching each other. Will that help your real estate investments?"

"I have none. Just my house. What little I've accumulated is in nontaxable state bonds. I receive a smaller yield on tax-exempt bonds as compared to a higher required yield on taxable bonds. So I guess we'll all have to be confused together. This turn of events simply mystifies me."

The sheriff shrugged. "I'm out of questions. All yours, Tim."

The youthful investigator folded his hands and looked at the attorney. "Mr. Grant, to the slight extent that the mists are clearing, it begins to seem as though a financial motive is behind both recent deaths. Can you think of anybody who would benefit handsomely from gaining three or more pieces of property along the Old Nelson Road?"

"No I can't. It's decent farmland, but it wouldn't make somebody filthy rich even if he had five or six of the properties out there. Why kill for such a modest return? Why not rob a bank?"

"Mr. Grant, could there be somebody in the background who feels he has an anointed right to own that land? Was it all part of a giant estate at one time?"

"I don't think so. It's been years and years since the land was divided into its present configurations. I've never heard of any disinherited party who wants to get something back."

"And the note threatening Douglas? You've seen that?"

"Yes. He sent me a copy of it. Surely it's just a bad joke. Should my nephew die, no property would change hands. So that hardly fits into this other row of dominoes. Frankly, I'm not seeing any patterns here. I'm only seeing isolated absurdities that sometimes happen in life."

"Anything else?" asked the sheriff.

"Indeed so," Tim rejoined. "I'm not through yet. Mr. Grant, if you were to die in the near future, who would get your land?"

"Uh...my nephew."

"If you both died together? A plane crash, a poorly vented stove...who gets it then?"

"I've willed everything to Sheriff Kruger. He's the murderer." The attorney relit his pipe and winked at the sheriff. "Just a little humor. You're taking this so seriously. In actuality, Tim, an assortment of charities would get my liquidated estate through a testamentary trust."

"So if Douglas died before or simultaneously with you, all three properties---your place, Burk's, and Orick Farm---would be sold at a fair-market price. Is that accurate?"

"That's right."

"So a wealthy businessman---a Ling Sumoto or a Walter Rankin---could buy all three."

"It's not unthinkable."

"Which either man would do in a minute if he knew something we don't know. If, in fact, there is something within this small parcel of real estate that makes it extremely valuable."

"That holds up, too." Elston Grant leaned back and puffed on his pipe. "Now, Tim, can you tell us what this hidden treasure might be? Is there a lost diamond mine underneath these three adjacent lots?"

"That's where the trail grows cold."

"Too bad. I thought we were just on the verge of bagging the fox."

After several moments of silence the sheriff asked, "Well, is that it? Are we all through this time?"

"No we aren't," Martin responded. "Mr. Grant, you now own two more properties, and you say you haven't the foggiest idea what if anything would be making them valuable. This being the case, do you object to a thorough search of the Orick and Burk properties? I'm talking about digging, and metal detectors, and a thorough examination of the buildings."

"Well, as long as I'm not paying for it, and the searchers can keep from demolishing any sound structures, then I'd agree to it." Grant turned to the sheriff. "When does this expedition start work?"

"Probably never. We can't search just to be searching. We've got to know what we're looking for. Still in all, Martin, you raised a good point. Now, everybody, since we can always get together later, let's call it a morning."

Martin stood up and said, "Mr. Grant, I'll see you this afternoon with Mr. Sumoto."

"Sure thing. We have a lot of work to do."

Tim and Martin held their comments until they were seated inside the Zippa convertible.

Martin slipped a small sugarless mint inside his mouth. "You know, for just a moment there, I thought he was going to say, 'It's none of your business who gets my stuff when I'm gone.' Did you pick that up?"

"He may have thought it. But he's in such an awkward position that he could hardly afford to say it. I keep thinking that humor can be used as a lubricant---a way of passing off things you don't want to let stick."

Martin was silent for over a minute. Finally he ventured his evaluation. "Too smooth. Just a fraction too smooth. He may not be the killer, but he's probably hiding something. I'll try to get more information when I meet with Grant and Sumoto this afternoon."

"I'm with Mr. Rankin---it's still too early for guesses. But, if Grant is hiding something, surely he would lean on his nephew to get rid of our investigative efforts. Why don't we see if that's happened yet?"

The duo backtracked to Elston Grant's office and learned that Douglas was working in Woodsfield on this particular Saturday.

"Okay, let's divide up and get things done more quickly," Tim said as the young men once again stepped outside. "Luckily we brought both cars. You drive to Woodsfield and tell Douglas that we're feeling snoopier than ever. Make sure that he's already told his uncle about us. Spell it out: we'll tell Uncle Elston if Douglas hasn't---we're being paid from the Grant treasury. Then, logically, Douglas will either dismiss us or cheer us on. Either way, we learn something, don't we?"

"Yes. We do."

"I'll stay here and wait for Verna Barger to show up."

"Then I'll hit the road. Anything else?" Martin asked.

"Yeah, there is. I want to find out who, if anyone, witnessed this codicil to Mrs. Burk's will."

"Kruger would know. I'll breeze by there on my way out of town. Since we've got tomorrow morning open, couldn't we track down that old friend of Sid Burk's who was arrested with him thirteen years ago?"

"If he's still alive and anywhere around here. Well, see you later. I'll be home by three, if you need me."

"Fine. See you this evening."

It was an hour later when Verna Barger returned to her real estate office on the southeast corner of Adams and New Jersey streets. A determined sleuth was waiting to question her.

"So you don't think your uncle drilled old Sid full of lead, huh?" ventured the outspoken broker. "Well, neither do I. But the cacklers in the henhouse haven't forgotten how to gossip. I'm afraid the idle tongues who know the least about it are the most likely to jump to conclusions, and harbor bad feelings toward your uncle and aunt."

"I feel the same way," Tim said. "Therefore it makes sense to find the person responsible as quickly as I can."

"Good luck."

Tim reiterated what had been said in Grant's office concerning the properties along Old Nelson Road. "You're familiar with land values and the potential uses of local land. What could make two or three properties valuable enough to kill for?"

"In my opinion, nothing. Either you're dealing with a psychopath, or there's something still to come to light."

A new thought crossed Tim's mind. "How about the location itself? I mean, with the river and all, could there be some state engineering project that we've not heard about? Or a new highway bridging over to West Virginia?"

"The way I hear it, this Rankin fellow has already looked into that, only a few minutes ahead of some deputy sheriff. But they both came up empty handed."

"Mrs. Barger, have you known for some time that Sid Burk owned Orick Farm?"

"Yes. Since March, anyway."

"You learned of it by accident?"

"Of course not. Sid Burk came here to my office, told me that he owned Orick Farm, and with Mrs. Orick's recent passing, wanted to sell it."

"You'll forgive me for saying so, I trust, but as forthright real estate people go, you've been very tightlipped about who owned that property. Mr. Sumoto didn't know. Furthermore, I can't find anyone else who knew the true state of affairs."

"Well, there's a reason for that, young man. Mr. Burk asked me to keep his ownership as mum as possible."

"Did he say why?"

"Not in so many words, but it's easy enough to figure. Sid Burk dressed poor, lived poor and took advantage of that image. He had lots of folks giving him stuff just because they thought he was poor and needed it. Now to own a second house, free and clear, spoils the pudding, don't you see? Also, deep pockets draw more thieves and lawsuits."

"I believe I do see. In other words, when you dealt with Mr. Sumoto, you said things like 'the owner wants this' or 'the owner plans that' to avoid saying 'Sid Burk owns Orick Farm.' Isn't that it?"

"That is it. That's one dark paper bag that you've successfully punched your way out of, Dr. Whinney."

"I thought Sid Burk was poor. Have you any idea where he found the money to buy Orick Farm?"

"Yes, I have an idea or two about that. First of all, Mrs. Orick didn't ask an arm and a leg for the place. Sid Burk was a tight spender with few vices and a house to live in that his parents had paid for. Finally, when Sid's father died, there was twenty thousand or so that went to Sid directly, although Molly got a nice chunk as well. So that pretty much explains it."

"I suppose so. There would have been no federal estate taxes. Mrs. Barger, did you know Sid Burk well?"

"No. Not well at all."

"Did anybody on earth know him well?"

"Probably not. He impressed me as a loner."

"Do you have the remotest idea as to why he was killed?"

"I surely don't. It's not my intention to knock holes in your highflying kite, Dr. Whinney, but have you considered the possibility that ten years from now you may still be completely in the dark as to who killed that man?"

"I certainly hope not," Tim frowned.

"Since you're an accounting professor, I have a question for you. What is the latest date for the replacement of similar property in an involuntary conversion of condemned real estate? Two years from the date of the realization of the gain?"

Tim paused and then stated, "I teach governmental accounting, not taxation. I would have to look it up. Sorry."

"No problem."

"Has some of the property involved with these murders been condemned?" Tim inquired.

"Oh, no. Just *another* client with a problem."

* * *

In Woodsfield, Martin located the law firm where Douglas Grant worked part-time as a paralegal. They stepped out for coffee, and in the tranquil setting of a small diner, Martin asked the questions he had brought from Greenharbor.

"Doug, does your uncle know that Tim and I are being paid by you to find Sid Burk's murderer?"

"Yes he does."

"Has he any objections?"

Martin could see a trace of tightness in the young man's face as Douglas responded. "No, but what would it matter if he did? I'm paying you with *my* money. I assure you that my uncle has a desire to keep me alive."

"I don't doubt it. Doug, I was surprised to discover that the two witnesses to the amendment of Molly Burk's will were you and some woman named Jane Potter. The codicil was dated four days ago, and yet your uncle only learned last night, from another attorney, about this rather incriminating inheritance. Now what in the world is going on?"

"Nothing that should upset you or Tim, or that would change our relationship. Look, my uncle got back from Cleveland very late last night. Then he left for his office earlier than usual, and we simply missed each other. Of course I wanted to explain that codicil to him, but we had no chance to talk. It can be most difficult to catch up to him at times."

"Okay. What happened on Tuesday the thirtieth?"

"Molly Burk called me. She asked if I would bring a friend and come to Barnesville to her apartment. She said it was legal business."

"Did she explain why she didn't care to use her own attorney, who lived in the same town she did?"

"No. Other than that...apparently she wanted to make a nice surprise out of the whole thing. Had my uncle been in Greenharbor last Tuesday, I think she would've invited him to drive up, and told him that he was her new heir, so he could sell the land and use the money for charity. I'm not sure if you know it, Martin, but my uncle is deeply involved in some charities and beneficent foundations in Greenharbor."

"So she asked for him, but accepted you as a stand-in?"

"That's right."
"Was she in some kind of hurry?"
"Not really. She had decided to do it, and once her mind was set, she wanted to get it on paper."
"So Jane was your guest?"
"Yes."
"Why her in particular?"
"Well...Mrs. Burk said to bring two signers, or two people over twenty-one...something like that. Believe me, Martin, as a paralegal I've had much stranger phone calls and requests than that one."
"Hmmm. I suppose...if she had gone on living, it wouldn't seem all that unusual. After all, her only son was dead...she had to do something with that property, in terms of a will..."
"That's right. That's exactly how I saw it. Everyone needs a will. Stories are legion about the disastrous consequences of dying intestate. By that I mean...dying without a will. In such a case, the state of Ohio tells how her assets would be distributed---a will by default."
"I know; I know." Martin almost shouted. "There's an old saying: where there's no will, there's no way."
"It was only last night that I heard of her death. Then, around lunchtime today, I got word that Tim suspected foul play...and it dawned on me that all of a sudden my uncle was placed in a suspicious light."
"Certainly. Doug, what about Jane? Will she verify all of this, when and if the sheriff asks?"
"Yes. Here...I'll give you her phone number and address. Gosh... I hope she hasn't left yet...she said something about a trip."
Martin finished his coffee as Douglas wrote out the information.
"I hope this clears it up for you, Martin. I want to emphasize, and to make it most distinct, that I did what happened to seem right at the time. If I've only managed to cloud the issue, or encouraged you to distrust me, then I'm sorry."
Martin looked at Douglas and wondered how much fear and apprehension might be trapped beneath the ice of his placid demeanor.
"I feel I can trust you, Doug. I'm sure Tim shares my feelings."
"That's good. Oh, by the way. Tell him to press on, and please give him this check for two hundred dollars. I...don't mean to sound paranoid, but sometimes I get the sensation...the awareness...that somebody in Greenharbor is watching me."
"Any more notes?"

"No. But things seem restless for me...uneven..." He paused as a waitress refilled his coffee cup, then left.

"We'll keep moving. Thanks for this address...and the money will be put to good use." Douglas Grant took several moments to gather his concluding thoughts. "I can't talk about my concerns with just anyone...but thank goodness you and Tim are involved in it now, and want to help me. I don't want anything to come between me and the two of you. I'd feel terrible if that happened. Maybe that's what somebody somewhere wants, but the thought of it chills me. Each day I count on you to...well, I'll just say it...I count on you to keep me alive."

Martin's next stop was Elston Grant's office in Greenharbor, to begin the real purpose of the trip to Greenharbor--the possible audit of the city.

Elston Grant shook hands with Martin and also greeted Ling Sumoto. Grant and Sumoto were members of the audit committee for the city of Greenharbor. "Have a seat, Martin." Grant motioned toward an empty seat. Looking at Ling, Grant said, "Martin is here to review our audit needs, as you know."

"Thank you, Mr. Grant. State law mandates an annual financial audit and a number of other requirements. The Single Audit Act has additional federal requirements," Martin said. "I've reviewed your current financial statements and the management letter issued by last year's auditor. The analysis seems incomplete, since there are comprehensive federal requirements. For example, the Single Audit Act requires reports on internal control and compliance. However, I don't have access to the previous auditor's working papers. They're subject to review by the federal government, but the results are confidential. I need to make a systems review before submitting a bid. Are there any contingencies I should be made aware of?"

"Well," stated an embarrassed Sumoto, "there may be a problem. Our revenues are smaller than they should be, especially in the utility fund. We increased water rates, but revenues still don't cover costs. Someone may be embezzling funds."

"That's great!" said an exasperated Martin. "Do you have any suspects?"

"Well no. But it seems logical that it's a problem in utility operations or data processing. Bill Mason runs the utility and has worked for the city almost 20 years. Stan Waterman is in charge of our computer operations. He's only been here about 18 months, but has a reputation as a programming wizard. Both men have a number of staff people that have access to the financial records."

"I'll have to review your computer control systems carefully. If it's okay, let me spend this afternoon analyzing the control systems at city hall."

* * *

Afterward Martin drove to city hall, an ancient building probably built at the turn of the century. It gave the city's operations that antiquated look, Martin thought, like their books were still being recorded with quill and ink by a descendant of Bob Cratchit. Martin was taken on an in-depth tour by Sally Reed, the finance director. The administrative and financial records were in the basement as were the computer and data processing operations. All the basic financial data were in computer storage, and most records were printed out on a monthly basis. Certain records that had frequent activity such as taxes and fines receivable were printed out daily.

Martin began reviewing the documentation available on the computer system, the existing internal controls, and the basic flows of data from the accounting system. The system was fairly simple, as expected for a small town. A single type of computer handled all data processing. There was no networking, no on-line terminals, but auditing the system would be fairly straight forward.

Clerks prepared input records to be entered into the computer and cashiers handled the cash receipts. All checks written required the signatures of both the vouchers payable clerk and the director of finance and required supporting documentation. The internal controls built into the system were limited, largely because of the small staff involved, but should have been adequate. An embezzler would need lackadaisical enforcement of the rules. Data diddling, for example, would require changing data before or during computer input. This diddling is possible, thought Martin, if the people approving the entries didn't review the documents carefully. Martin made a mental note to check all large dollar amount vouchers. On the other hand, if the villain was the computer manager, the crime would be more difficult to detect. Embezzlement could involve "elegant" utility programs.

The city's accounting system had 15 individual funds, each an independent accounting system with its own journals and ledgers and separate financial reports. Special care would be needed for the Pension Trust Fund and the two proprietary funds. Too bad the city didn't join the state's retirement plan, thought Martin. Then the pension problems would be the headache of the state auditor's office. The water utility problem was going to require some additional planning. Also, the Data Processing Internal Service Fund might be involved. The use of fund accounting would require Martin to prepare separate audit programs for each fund type.

Martin completed his systems review and decided to submit a bid under $10,000, a high price for a city this size. However, the potential for fraud and new federal audit requirements meant that this might be a substandard fee. At a normal billing rate of $100 per hour, a 100 hour audit would be standard. But actual hours could greatly exceed this target.

With his plan developed, Martin went to Elston Grant's office. Sally also was there. "I'll submit a bid under $10,000. This assumes that I can get some help from your staff and find no additional problem areas. If I find evidence of fraud, I'll turn that information over to you and the county attorney. Hopefully, this shouldn't add to the cost of the audit."

"That sounds great to us, Martin," said Sally. "Your work comes highly recommended."

Grant interjected, "I'll call the audit committee members of the city council for informal approval today. A week from Tuesday is the last day of the fiscal year. Can you start the audit within the next three weeks?"

"No problem. I'll prepare an engagement letter and have it on your desk by tomorrow. The engagement letter will detail our rights and obligations with the audit. The procedures we'll have to follow if fraud is discovered will be more detailed than usual, but this detail is important if your suspicions of fraud are correct. See you tomorrow."

* * *

After Martin completed the engagement letter for the Greenharbor audit, he called Elston Grant on the phone. "Hi Elston, this is Martin Zippa. I've finished the engagement letter and can be at your office by two. Is that all right with you?"

"That's great, Martin. The city council has approved your audit and you can start working any time."

"Good," continued Martin. "I'll need a workroom. If your accounting staff will cooperate, I'll borrow the financial statements and various documents as I need them. Sometime in the next couple of weeks I'll make a surprise visit to count the cash and review all negotiable instruments. Please, don't tip anybody off. The element of surprise is a necessary part of that phase of the audit. See you this afternoon."

After arriving at city hall that afternoon, Martin reviewed the contents of the engagement letter with John Miller, the City Manager. "This will be a financial and compliance audit that will satisfy single audit regulations. It will cover all funds for the fiscal year. The audit will begin within two weeks after the accounts are closed and financial statements prepared. The target date for completion is two months after the audit begins. I will prepare an auditor's opinion to be included with the city's comprehensive annual financial report and several other reports that must be filed with the state auditor and the federal government. The cognizant audit agency is the Department of Housing and Urban Development and I will contact them before the audit starts and work closely with them. The financial statements must be based on GAAP and the audit procedures will use generally accepted auditing standards and generally accepted government auditing standards, which are based on the *Yellow Book* ..."

"Whoa," said John. "I'm no accountant. Slow down and explain some of those terms. What's a cognizant audit agency and what are these auditing standards you're talking about?"

"Well," stated Martin, reviewing the engagement letter carefully so that John would understand all aspects of the contract, "the cognizant audit agency is a federal agency or department that is responsible for reviewing the audit reports and ensuring that any deficiencies are corrected. There is a sharing arrangement so that most of the departments split these duties. For example, the Department of Education handles mostly school districts. HUD is your cognizant audit agency, although I haven't the foggiest idea why.

"This is a requirement of the Single Audit Act. The federal government is involved primarily because of the $100 billion plus they spend annually in grants to state and local governments. The idea is to demand that these monies are spent according to the law--that's why the compliance procedures--and the audits are done efficiently. That's why uniform procedures are required. Essentially, the cognizant audit agency audits the auditor."

"I see, Martin. Now what about these audit standards?"

Martin continued, "There are two sets. First, there are generally accepted auditing standards or GAAS. As a CPA I must follow GAAS for any audit engagement. A governmental audit is similar to one for a commercial firm, but there are some additional rules. These include generally accepted government auditing standards or GAGAS. GAGAS were developed by the General Accounting Office in *Government Auditing Standards* which is sometimes called the *Yellow Book*.

"These federal requirements mean more hours are needed to complete the job. I'll have to evaluate your internal control system and submit a report on my findings. I also have to test compliance with the laws and regulations associated with each major federal assistance program and write a report on that."

"So, you'll claim that your fee is a real bargain for the amount of work involved."

"You better believe is," stated Martin emphatically. "At the end of the engagement, I'll write a management letter which will review my evaluation of the accounting system, internal controls, and so on, and state my recommendations for improvements. This report will be prepared for you and the city council and I'll be happy to present it at a meeting. There are lots of details in the engagement letter, including a termination clause, duties if fraud is detected, and so on. I'll review those with Sally. Do you have any questions?"

"What about our revenue shortfalls?"

"I have no opinion yet. The audit is not specifically designed to detect fraud. But I'll look carefully. If there's fraud, it's likely we'll find it. If there's collusion, it may be harder to detect. I have guidelines to detect fraud under Statement of Auditing Standards 53. There's a good chance we'll solve this problem."

"Look Martin, we are having an executive committee meeting on a proposed new tax in an hour. I want you to attend and you'll get to meet some of our employees."

"No problem; I'll be glad to attend."

* * *

About an hour later Martin heard John Miller, the city manager of Greenharbor, open the executive committee meeting.

"Under a bill passed by the state last year, cities could voluntarily charge a one percent sales tax on all purchases made within the boundaries of the city, beginning on January 1," John began. "This would substantially increase the city's revenues in future years if approved by the city council. The purpose of our meeting is to make recommendations to the city council on whether or not to implement the sales tax and, if so, what to do with the additional revenues.

"Sally's the budget expert," said John. "I've asked her to prepare some revenue forecasts and present some options for using the tax revenue."

Sally Reed, as the director of finance, had spent considerable time preparing her report. "Under the state's system the sales tax will be collected by the State Treasurer and our share will be rebated to us quarterly," Sally began. "That means we should start receiving cash in the fourth quarter of next fiscal year, probably around $30,000. The following year we project total sales tax collections of $240,000, which will increase to over $300,000 annually within five years. Last year's General Fund revenue was $921,000 and is expected to reach $1,000,000--excluding the sales tax--within two years. So, by next year, a sales tax could increase General Fund revenues over 25%. The tax will rise and fall with the business cycle and can be hard to forecast in a specific quarter. Long-term, however, it represents a reasonably stable resource. We have two basic choices if the sales tax is approved. Other taxes can be cut or spending can be increased."

"Or we can do both," interjected John.

"Right. We can do both," said Sally. "In fact, our choices are even broader than that. For example, we can maintain current revenues but avoid new tax increases if spending rises. There's plenty of flexibility."

"I think we should raise salaries and increase police recruit training," said Sheriff Kruger.

"No, property taxes should be cut," stated Jerry Abbott, the budget director.

"Well, I believe we should reduce water utility rates," said John Miller. "What about a compromise? We cut property tax rates and still increase appropriations where we need them. Sally, please run some projections. Let's assume that property tax rates are cut five percent."

"Give me a minute," said Sally, "and I'll have the property tax numbers." Sally pulled out her calculator and revenue summary data and went to work. In no time the calculations were complete. "In the forthcoming year the tax rate is 70 cents per $100 net assessed value and NAV is $120 million. That gives us a tax levy of $840,000. Current collections should be 94% or about $790,000 plus delinquent collections of $32,000. A five percent cut in the rate would give us a tax rate of 66.5 cents on a projected NAV of $124 million. The tax levy would be almost $825,000. With the same collection rate and delinquent collections of $32,500, revenue would be $808,000, a drop of $14,000 from this year and a drop of a bit over $40,000 from next year's revenue using the same 70 cent tax rate. That $40,000 tax cut would leave $200,000 for increased appropriations, assuming we use the $240,000 forecast of sales tax revenues for next year. If we cut the tax rate by ten percent, the tax cut would be about $81,000, which would leave almost $160,000 to increase spending. There are other ways to calculate the cuts. Shall I consider any more alternatives?"

"Thanks Sally," said John. "That's enough for now."

John turned to Jerry Abbott, "Jerry, develop new budget request forms contingent on the sales tax; use a zero-based budget format so that we get specific decision packages that can be ranked. Let's get the forms out today to all department heads and request they be returned next week. We need to nail down some numbers to make a good presentation to the city council."

"ZBB for all spending or just new funding?" questioned Jerry.

"Just the new funding. Line item budgeting works well for current spending levels. We just need to adjust for growth and inflation. But additional spending needs substantial documentation for approval by the city council."

John looked around the room and everyone appeared to be as ready to move on as he was. "Let's get together with Jerry next week, after we have the budget requests and consider all our options. Until then, we have work to do."

John Miller picked up the memo from Sally Reed on GASB Statement No. 11. "According to a memo from Sally, the city's administration needs to think about the implications of the new measurement focus and its impact on city financial operations." Sometimes John regretted not paying more attention in the accounting courses he took in his MBA program.

"Sally, would you explain to the group why this Measurement Focus/Basis of Accounting Statement is important? The effective date was supposed to begin for fiscal years starting after June 15, 1994 with early application not permitted. But the effective date has been postponed. It may still be years away."

"You're right, John; we have plenty of time to prepare for the MFBA changes. My point is, let's anticipate the impact and plan accordingly. This statement has some effect on most of the operations in the governmental funds. The revenue recognition criteria are different. The Statement requires the consumption method for supplies. We now use the purchase method."

"Slow down, Sally. I'm not seeing the problems. Let's go through these one at a time. What about supplies?" John had a puzzled look on his face.

"We'll have to switch to the consumption method, just like we use in the Enterprise Fund. Not a big deal. The consumption method is allowed under current GAAP; we can switch any time," Sally responded.

"Any problems?" asked John.

"Not really. This switch does not affect cash flows and won't change our inventory procedures much. The expenditures for supplies will have to be booked when they're used by the departments rather than when received. We can make an adjusting entry at year-end and switch."

"That doesn't seem difficult; are compensated absences still a problem?" asked John.

"Fortunately, compensated absences are *not* a problem," stated Sally. We've already changed from cash basis to accrual because of GASB Statement No. 16. We recognize expenditures and liabilities in the General Fund for accrued vacation pay and sick leave. That's the reason we raised the property tax rates last year, to cover these new expenditures and still have a balanced budget."

"Okay, but what about taxes?" asked John quickly.

"A minor headache. The most significant impact will be on property taxes. The present system of revenue recognition comes reasonably close to matching cash inflows to revenues. The new approach matches revenue recognition to the current tax levy and penalty charges. The MFBA method emphasizes interperiod equity."

"What's the difference, Sally?"

"The difference is that revenue recognition is no longer directly related to cash flows. For example, about five percent of the tax levy becomes delinquent, but we end up collecting about 80% of the delinquent taxes. Under current GAAP we recognize the 95% as revenue and expected current year collections of delinquencies. Under the MFBA approach, 99% of the tax levy--all but bad debts--is revenue this year. Also, we charge a three percent penalty on delinquent taxes and record most of that as deferred revenues, because we'll collect all but bad debts in future years. Under MFBA the amount collectible is revenue this year, regardless of when cash is collected."

"But won't revenue recognition even out from one year to the next?" John suggested.

"Generally." said Sally. "But cash flows can be erratic. In our budgeting procedures we want a balanced budget and that relates appropriations to estimated revenues, not estimated cash flows. The new approach is based on solid accounting concepts, but watching cash flows will be a bit more difficult. It is interesting that we will be able to continue using cash basis for fines and forfeitures. That's allowed under Statement 11, since actual amounts are so difficult to forecast. If the city council approves the new sales tax, revenue recognition shouldn't be much of a problem. Sales tax with a due date of 60 days after the end of the fiscal year will have to be accrued. The last quarter's tax will have to be based on forecasts, but its doable."

"This is complicated," exclaimed a shocked John. "I guess we do need a few years to prepare. What's the next step?"

"I suggest a contingency plan. We should convert inventories to the consumption method at year-end. I'll further analyze the effect on taxes and try to forecast the problems with revenue recognition changes and maintaining a balanced budget. We don't have all the answers since new pronouncements must be issued by the GASB. No reason to do something rash."

John held up his hands. "Okay. Okay. The meeting is adjourned."

Chapter Eleven

Performance audits follow the established pattern of financial audits, but they also include an examination, conducted under established auditing standards, of the degree to which management is achieving desired results. These results are evaluated by examining the efficiency and economy of resource use, the effectiveness of the achievement of desirable objectives, and the compliance with legal and regulatory requirements.
J. Gregory Bushong
Robert L. Belk

As Tim drove northward out of Greenharbor, he noticed the Ohio River to his right. It reminded him of the chalkboard stream he often drew for his students. The stream, which represented a person's inflow of wealth, flowed into one's gross taxable income lake. Along the stream were three dams: statutes, definition and constitution.

These dams allowed water to flow away from the gross taxable income lake into nontaxable smaller streams. For example, by statutes certain business meals and lodging expenses were tax-free. So too were gifts and inheritance. By definition, a person's investment in an asset was not taxable. In other words, when a taxpayer sold some stock shares, his or her investment was a return of capital, and therefore not taxable. The smallest dam was the constitution. Interest on certain governmental obligations was not taxable. However, any gain on such obligations would be taxable.

Tim's thoughts returned to more current concerns as he turned right onto Old Nelson Road, passed his uncle's house, and finally rolled to a stop beneath the thick growth of trees that separated Shawn Sparlin's house from the roadway. The house itself was small, trim and clean. Tim wondered what it would be like to live by oneself in such a rustic setting. He knocked on the door. Before long, Shawn Sparlin opened the door. Although he was Tim's age, the young black musician seemed a good deal younger. He was wearing blue jeans and a light blue t-shirt.

"Hello, neighbor," Tim said with a smile. "I thought maybe we could have a little visit."

"Yeah, I'd like that. Come in."

They took seats in the comfortable but modest living room. "Tim, you remember how you used to visit my dorm room and play my guitar? It took forever to tune it after you messed with it."

Tim laughed. "I must have been a pest."

"Those were the days," Shawn said with a sigh. "Say, do you still play poker?"

"Yeah...a little."

"Bring Martin over and we'll play four-handed---you two, me and a pal of mine named Harry. How about Monday night?"

"Great." Tim admired some wooden statues that Shawn had carved by hand, and then moved to his main topic. "Shawn, did you know Sid Burk very well?"

"No, man. He kept to himself."

"Do you have any ideas on why he was killed?"

"Greed."

Tim smiled. "Quite possibly. But *whose* greed?"

"If I knew anything, I'd tell you. And if I learn anything, I'll get in touch right away."

"Please do." Tim stood up. "After all, I'm just down the road."

Shawn stepped into the tree-covered front yard with Tim. "There's a pond between my house and the river. Never runs dry, not even in the worst of summer. And the trees around it keep the sun away. It's my favorite place---the reason I wouldn't sell Sparlin Farm, even after Momma and Papa died. Want to see it?"

Tim shrugged. "Why not?"

Together they made their way past a back yard full of apple trees, down one small hill and up another, and through a copse of green branches.

"Hey, man, there ain't no pond here!" Tim complained jocularly. "The river's only about five feet away."

"Pond first, river next," Shawn replied as he stopped at a huge oak tree and gestured beyond it with his left hand.

Tim stepped around the oak tree and came into view of a sparkling blue pond with sandy banks and a small wooden pier at one end. "God... it's beautiful!" He looked back at his host. "You swim here?"

Shawn smiled. "*We'll* swim here. With a few selected guests. One of them could be Martin."

"Sounds delightful. When do we try out the pond?"

"Anytime. Bring your swimwear and come over anytime. Can you scuba dive?"

"No, but I've always wanted to take lessons."

"Good. I'm a scuba instructor and I'll teach you," suggested Shawn.

"A great idea," said Tim. "I'll talk to Martin and see if he wants to learn."

* * *

Martin made his way through the dimly lit bar to the table where only one man sat, working his way into a third beer. The seated man appeared to be in his late thirties.

"My friend the bartender says you might be Ed Colyer." Martin tossed out the words in a breezy, amicable manner.

"Funny how right a bartender can be." Colyer motioned toward an empty chair. "Have a seat."

"Thanks."

"I'm Ed." His hand reached out. "Who might you be?"

"My name's Martin Zippa." They shook hands. "I was hoping we could talk just a minute about an old friend of yours---Sid Burk."

"Sid? Never did have all that close a friendship with the man."

"But he was good for a beer now and then?"

"Oh, yeah. Sure. Well, Sid used to drink quite a bit. Back when we were younger. Course he couldn't keep up with me."

"I'll bet not."

"Quiet fellow. Never chased women. Never chased money. Just a floater, you might say."

Martin let a few seconds roll by without any conversation. Then, softly and matter-of-factly, he moved toward his point. "About thirteen years ago, Sid had a little run-in with the law at a wood stove factory near Clarington."

A wry smirk crossed Colyer's face. "Well...a lot of water's flowed down the Ohio since then. You, uh...checkin' out a job application for Sid, Mr. Zippa?"

"You can call me Martin. It sounds as if...I need to give you some bad news. Sid Burk was murdered on the twenty-fifth of May."

Colyer seemed surprised. "Murdered? Who did it?"

"We don't know. The killer is still loose, and I'm employed by someone who might become the next victim."

"Hmmm. It's hard to believe Sid's gone."

"It's difficult to know ahead of time just which piece of information will trip up the murderer. But you can help me, Mr. Colyer, and perhaps aid in catching Sid Burk's killer. Now...the break-in at the stove factory...what happened?"

Ed Colyer took a long, slow drink of beer. "We were young. We'd had too much to drink. One or the other of us hit on the idea of prowlin' through the stove plant. Lookin' for money or tools or who knows what. We were too drunk to know what we wanted. They didn't have a watchman, but the sheriff's department made regular checks. They saw us, but we got through the fence and ran away. About twenty minutes later they found us down the road, and took us in."

"No prosecution?"

"Well by some miracle we didn't leave any clues, and we both swore we were innocent. The prosecutor said he didn't have a case, and dismissed it. That was that."

"Nobody else involved? No third party?"

"Nope. Just a silly mistake."

"Then as far as you know, that was Sid Burk's one and only crime?"

"If you could call that a crime. Sid was a good fellow...never hurt anyone. I'm sorry to hear that he's gone."

"I'm afraid he is, and his killer isn't, and therein lies my task."

"Heck of a thing. Could I buy you a beer, Mr. Zippa...uh, Martin, was it?"

"I think I could go along with that, Mr. Colyer."

Chapter Twelve

GAAP classifies funds in governmental units into three broad categories--governmental funds, proprietary funds, and fiduciary funds. Governmental funds (the General Fund, Special Revenue Funds, Capital Project Funds and Debt Service Funds) differ from funds in other categories because of their focus on expenditures.
Shari H. Wescott
Stanley Y. Chang

On Sunday afternoon Tim and Lisa paid a visit to Walter Rankin at the Greenharbor Motel.

"Very glad to see you," his friendly voice boomed. "Any new leads?"

The three of them placed their chairs in a triangular formation. Tim leaned forward in his chair.

"Nothing really solid. With an absolute maximum of eight suspects, you'd think somebody would emerge as a prime magnet for our suspicion. But it isn't happening."

"At the same time," mused Rankin, "the sheriff's theory that one of the eight is either knowledgeable or personally guilty seems unbreakably strong. I've looked at it sideways, backwards, and upside down. Even went so far as to check on the integrity of the deputies watching the road. It's solid, Tim. No flim-flam anywhere."

"How is your *personal* investigation doing?" Lisa asked their host.

"Well, now that you mention it, I've devoted some of my spare time to local geography. Why don't you folks take a look at this map I've fixed up?"

Using the bed as a table, Rankin produced an enlargement of a hand-drawn map that outlined the four pieces of property north of the Whinney farm. Added coloring on the map marked Sid Burk's property, Orick Farm, and Elston Grant's property.

"If you could add Sparlin Farm to this little empire, you'd have a very nice chunk of real estate, wedged between a major highway and the river. It's a choice site because the Sparlin and Burk properties have a high bankline against the river, and never flood."

"Are you by any chance suggesting," Tim wondered out loud, "that Elston Grant would benefit immensely if he came into control of all four quarters of this land?"

"That's right. The four pieces together would be big enough to develop for any number of commercial uses."

"Still in all," Lisa added, "that's not enough to convince a jury that Elston Grant killed anybody."

"No, of course not," Rankin agreed. "But at least we can see a motive emerging, when before nobody could think of any reason for Burk being killed."

Tim studied the map closely. "But surely, if it's Elston Grant, he wouldn't dare move to develop the property anytime soon."

"He might, if he can cast enough suspicion on your uncle. Forewarned is forearmed, Tim. Your uncle and aunt had better expect some more bad publicity. I doubt the next move will be as clumsy as the rusty toolbox fiasco."

Tim nodded. "I tend to agree with you. By the way, Mr. Rankin, I understand you're leaving town."

"Yes, for a few days. I have to handle some business in Cincinnati. But I'll be back, possibly with reinforcements. When I do get back to Greenharbor, perhaps you and Lisa would like to drive down and see this amusement park I'm going to own a share of. We could all drive down there for a day or two, as a holiday of sorts."

"Sounds like a great idea to me," Lisa replied for both of them.

* * *

The first Monday in June was a sunny, breezy day filled with the fragrance of late spring and promising a tropical summer ahead. As Martin parked his convertible in front of the Greenharbor Little Theater, he glanced toward the sun, and felt its warmth soaking through his shirt. This kind of weather was highly compatible with his plan to maintain a deep tan from head to toe. Inside the theater, darker and cooler than the outdoors, he wasted no time in finding Novia Dixon.

"Martin! I'm glad to see you!"

"Thanks. I had some new questions, so I thought maybe you'd be willing to talk with me over coffee."

"Sure. There's a small coffee shop two doors down. We can get a quiet table. How about that?"

"Fine."

Ten minutes later, as she sipped coffee and he nursed a glass of orange juice, they talked.

"Who's Jane Potter?"

"A friend," she answered without hesitation. "A very good friend. Do you know her?"

"No, I don't. Her name has come up because she and Douglas Grant are the two witnesses who signed their names to Molly Burk's final amendment to her will. I've talked to Doug and he assures me that the transfer of the Burk property to Elston Grant was entirely Molly's idea. In fairness to all concerned, and for the sake of conducting a competent investigation, I'd like to verify Molly's comments with Jane. Do you know where she is?"

"No...in fact, it's been several days since I saw her. She told me last month that she planned to do some traveling this summer. Mentioned seeing her grandparents, who live in Canada."

"So she might be out-of-state."

"Possibly. But normally she would stop by and see us before she takes a long trip."

"Then she's active in theater here?"

"Somewhat active, yes."

"If you see her, Novia, please tell her that I'd like to talk with her."

"I'll be happy to." Novia took another swallow of her coffee. "Are you trying to avoid saying that you distrust Douglas's story?"

"I'm not saying that. I like Doug, and my inclination is to believe him. But if I were an attorney, I wouldn't dare go to court and say that I just assumed a material witness would say such-and-such, so I never questioned her. It's called covering your...uh...bases."

"Right. Quite improper to let anyone see an uncovered...base."

Martin finished the orange juice. "Anything else new? Any rumors I should hear?"

"Well, I hear little about crime. There's a rumor that our theater season will be extraordinary. You might want to investigate that."

"I'd like to." He smiled at her. "I'd even like to be in one of your plays, but my other commitments rule it out."

"I understand. Still in all, we can always use an extra hand. For example, our second production will be an Ohio playwright's work about the Greek gods. There's a lot of first-time costuming involved, and...how shall I put this...a lot of our male performers are reluctant to test skimpy costumes."

"You need a body to drape some costumes on."

"Exactly. A male body that can help us visualize what works, what doesn't, what needs another small strap..."

"Give me a ring if you need me. I've been seen in a g-string or less, and it doesn't embarrass me at all."

"Thanks. I wouldn't bring it up if the need weren't genuine."

On Monday afternoon, Tim and Martin met in the Whinney living room to compare notes. A large window fan brought them some relief from the heat, but it remained an uncomfortably warm day.

"I vote we buy an air conditioner," Martin said as he wiped the sweat off his forehead. "The radio predicted even hotter weather tomorrow."

"First we earn some money, and then we buy creature comforts. Tell me about Jane Potter."

"She's gone, apparently to Canada to visit relatives. Left in something of a hurry, according to her landlady."

"Surely somebody has an address or a phone number for her?"

"Surely not."

"Too bad."

"Novia will call me if Jane should phone or send a card or anything."

"Terrific. Changing the subject a little, what was Ed Colyer good for?"

"Ed was good for two beers and not much else. He admits they did it, but it was a drunken frolic of no consequence that I can discern."

"Planned or spontaneous?"

"I beg your pardon?"

"Did Burk and Colyer plan the break-in and then get drunk, or did they get drunk first and then try their luck..."

"Now I'm with you. The latter. A spur-of-the-moment act, as Colyer recalls it."

"Did you buy his credibility?"

"Yes."

"So what does that tell you about Burk?"

"Nothing. Absolutely nothing."

Tim paused to take a sip from a glass of iced tea. "Perhaps a little, Martin. Wasn't the impulsiveness of that bungled break-in worth noting? Isn't there a kick-in-the-dark, grab-the-necklace-and-never-mind-the-lady's-head-is-still-attached mentality in operation? If so, maybe that has a bearing on how Burk got himself killed, thirteen unlucky years later."

"Yes, that could be. Incidentally, for what little they're worth, I made extensive notes on my talk with Colyer and my background work on Potter. Do you by any remote chance want to read all of that?"

"Yes. Believe it or not, I want a copy of every word you've written, every document that comes our way, and every morsel of information we gather. I have a feeling that properly putting together the little things will give us the answers we need."

Tim and Martin enjoyed a tasty supper with Uncle Everett and Aunt Mildred. Then the young investigators excused themselves, to continue their work at Sparlin Farm.

By eight p.m. that evening, as the sunlight began to give way to electrical light, Tim and Martin sat in earnest but friendly combat with Shawn and his pal Harry, a pleasantly dispositioned young black who lived in Greenharbor and made his living as an auto mechanic.

"I'll see your Snickers bar, and raise you an Oh Henry," Tim told Shawn.

Harry looked again at his cards. "Uh-oh. This is getting serious. Okay. I'll see your Oh Henry and raise you a Baby Ruth."

The game continued for another hour, with Martin increasing his lead to the point that he had nine more candy bars than anyone else.

"If it's over a hundred degrees tomorrow," Martin observed, "then it won't matter who has the most loot. They're all gonna melt."

"No such thing," replied Shawn as he dealt out a fresh hand to everyone. "The bars will stay in the refrigerator, and we'll cool off by taking a swim. Which we should've done tonight."

There was a dull thud as some object struck the house. "Now there's that same noise again. Shawn, are you sure you don't have somebody prowling around out there?" Tim asked.

Curiosity overcoming inertia, Martin and Harry got up to see if there were any signs of intruders.

Shawn waited patiently for the game to resume. "Like I told you earlier, that's just Mr. Reaper. He's invited me to ride with him many a time, but I told him it'd be a few more days."

Tim glanced from his hand to his friend. "You're morbid, Shawn."

Martin and Harry returned to the table. "It's just the breeze," Martin declared. "That one tree's awfully close to the house, and the wind's been kicking up."

The game resumed. Shawn rallied briefly and won seven of Martin's candy bars, but eventually the Zippa tide swept everything clean, and all the candy went to Martin.

"Refreshment time," Shawn announced. "I've got some New Orleans drinks for everyone to try."

After two Cajun Zombies and three Delta Queens, Tim was ready to call it a night. "If nobody minds, I would like to crawl home."

Harry and Shawn looked up from their guitars. "You packin' it in?"

"I'm cashing in my chips. You coming, Mr. Candy Bar King?"

"Your chariot awaits," Martin replied.

"You guys can stay here," Shawn offered.

"Thanks. It's barely half a mile on a deserted country lane. We'll make it. Do I bring my trunks and towels tomorrow? And when's your pool open for business, Shawn?" Martin asked.

"I've got towels. And the pond's there twenty-four hours a day."

"We'll put it to good use."

* * *

Uncle Everett and Aunt Mildred had the tranquility of their evening interrupted by a visit from Wade Nagle and another deputy. With his usual disregard for pleasantries, he came promptly to the point.

"Mr. Whinney, I'm sure you can understand, with all the violence we've had around here, why we're keeping a close eye on new gun purchases."

Everett Whinney could think of no reply to that.

Eventually his wife volunteered, "How does that concern us, Deputy Nagle?"

"We were wondering why you would be purchasing a new rifle, Mr. Whinney. Planning to do some shooting, are you?"

"There must be some mistake. I haven't bought a firearm in over ten years."

"No mistake at all. Got your application right here. Your name, you rural box number. And a fine weapon it is. Good telescopic sight. Got any specific targets in mind, Mr. Whinney?"

Uncle Everett stared at the paper. "This is crazy. Somebody filled this out in my name. But it's a falsehood. I'm not buying this weapon."

The deputies glanced at each other. Nagle's voice became a grating mixture of falsetto and sarcasm. "Just as I thought, Joe. The Phantom Gun Purchaser has struck again." Returning to his normal tone, Nagle frowned at the Whinneys and tipped his hat. "Good evening, folks."

Chapter Thirteen

Our taxes reflect a continuing struggle among contending interests for the privilege of paying the least.
                              Louis Eisenstein

At the breakfast table, Tim threw another aspirin tablet into his orange juice. "If I've got this straight, Uncle Everett, we're talking about some gun dealer in Woodsfield."
"That's it. Dawson, the gun dealer. For some reason or other he turns in gun purchases to the sheriff. So here comes a piece of paper---stationery from Dawson, as I got the story---making me look like I'm arming myself to the teeth."
"What kind of weapon?" inquired Martin's soft voice.
"A Remington 552 with a telescopic sight."
"Hardly Nagle's business if we *were* buying one," Aunt Mildred injected tartly as she served some scrambled eggs. "But it's a lie, of course. A scheme by *somebody* out there to discredit your uncle."
Tim groaned. "So...what we're talking about is something hand lettered on a piece of paper. No eyewitness."
Uncle Everett finished his coffee. "Well, I'm driving over to Woodsfield this morning, and set Dawson straight. I want him to pass the word, in no uncertain terms, that he never talked to me about a rifle or any other weapon."
Uncle Everett asked Tim if he and Martin wanted to ride along. The offer was declined, on the theory that the task did not require four workers. Still in a huff over the sheriff's inability to recognize an obvious fraud, Uncle Everett and Aunt Mildred departed.
Martin winced as the last door slammed in the distance. "Oh...I thought they were never going to leave. My head...is in no condition for this noisy acrimony."
"You said it. Uh-h-h..." Tim put his head down on the table. "If the Delta Queen was going south, I should've gotten off at St. Louis."
"I should've gotten off at Minneapolis. Let's get some more sleep."
After two hours of additional rest, the young sleuths drove to Greenharbor and discussed the phony gun-purchase form with Sheriff Kruger.
"It just turned up on some deputy's desk. We

checked on it, and Dawson can't recall writing it."

"So it could be another piece in a fairly elaborate frame."

"A small piece...perhaps."

"It could get bigger quick," Martin suggested. "This establishes that Everett Whinney may have tried to buy a Remington 552. Suppose next week there's a robbery committed, using that type of gun. Then maybe it turns up in the Whinney barn."

"I guess it could happen, but I doubt it. Anyway, let me know if you fellows turn anything up."

Tim and Martin had lunch in Greenharbor, then tried to trace the Dawson memo to some source prior to a deputy's desk. This search produced no results.

As Tim walked back to the convertible, he noticed that his comrade had put the top up.

"What's this?" Tim slid into the passenger's seat. "No sun worship today?"

"Tim, it's ninety-eight. The humidity's up. And your house needs air conditioning." Martin started his car and turned on the air conditioner. "Let's go swimming at Shawn's. I like the idea of learning to scuba dive."

"Do we stop at the house for...towels?"

"I put towels and bathing trunks in my car this morning."

A few minutes later, the Zippa convertible rolled to a stop in the driveway of Sparlin Farm. Tim and Martin found Shawn sitting under a tree in his front yard, picking on his guitar.

"Good afternoon," Tim said. "Got any remote idea why we're here?"

"Sure. Let me stash the guitar and grab some blankets and stuff."

"Martin and I want to learn scuba diving," Tim said quickly.

"You know you have to take some classes and pass a written exam. I'm starting a new course this Saturday. Do you wish to attend? It'll cost you both $175," Shawn said.

"No problem," Tim said, looking at Martin.

Martin shook his head yes. "Is there anything we can do today in the pond?"

"Sure," Shawn said. "I can teach you how to put on the mask and snorkel. You can practice swimming with fins. Have you snorkled before?"

Martin had and Tim had not.

"I have some new force fins," Shawn said. "Tim can use them."

"What are force fins?" Martin asked.

85

"Force fins are designed to allow a more hydrodynamic finning stroke. The blades open on the power stroke and fold on recovery to reduce drag. Tim will use less energy and less air. Martin, you'll have to use conventional black fins. Sorry."

"Not a problem," Martin boasted. "I'm a good swimmer."

Each of the three took a handful of supplies, and they began the trek through the dense growth of trees, winding their way to the large oak tree that Tim remembered. They came into the circular clearing with the half-shaded pond, and Martin expressed his surprise at the beauty of the spot.

"Tim said the same thing," Shawn remarked as he dropped a blanket and his unbuttoned shirt, all in one motion.

Extremely tall trees stood guard on every side of the sparkling water. Despite the heat and humidity, a temperate breeze sifted through the trees and green foliage, tugging at Tim's loose shirt and turning it into a cape. The water rippled its invitation.

They changed clothes, put on fins, masks, and snorkels, and Shawn plunged into the pond first, closely followed by Martin.

"Come on in, Tim." It was a genial invitation.

In mere moments, the water's refreshment and the peacefulness of their private world combined to energize the swimmers. Tim could almost perceive an emotional bond interlacing the three of them.

* * *

On Wednesday, Ling Sumoto called the Whinney farmhouse to speak with Martin, and gave him the time of appointment with the city budgeting committee. The phone conversation led in turn to a personal conversation between Martin and the director of finance.

"Hi, Sally, this is Martin. I have a couple of questions on the accounting system. I'm working on the city's audit."

"Fire away, Martin."

"First, footnote seven from your annual report shows an accounting change in compensated absences, to accrual basis for vacation pay and sick leave. Can I assume that this is based on GASB Statement No. 16?"

"That's right," stated Sally. "We were planning to start accruals anyway, but this made us change over a year early."

"That's fine. Please say so in the footnote. Also, the disclosures are a little different from the Appendix

B illustration. If you can change the disclosure, I can avoid the chance of a qualified audit opinion. I've calculated some new tables."

"I would like to see your tables, but I don't anticipate any problems. I appreciate you finding that discrepancy," Sally said.

"Second, I couldn't find the schedule of federal financial assistance programs related documentation. I have to write a report on compliance with federal laws and regulations, and there are a number of audit procedures I'll have to make."

"Oh, I'm sorry, Martin. The department spend several weeks working on those federal program reports. The city attorney has the complete file."

"Okay," said Martin. "I'll make an appointment with him. In addition to those files I need a representation letter from him on any outstanding litigation and claims. I'll keep in touch. Thanks for your help, Sally."

While Martin was busy in Greenharbor, Tim paid a friendly visit to Dawson the gun dealer. The Woodsfield merchant was now fairly certain that he had not talked to Everett Whinney before Tuesday, and explained that almost anyone could have quietly pocketed one of the gun-purchase forms.

"The deputy showed me the slip. It was all marked up in pencil, and at first I thought it was mine. But the more I looked, the more I couldn't remember it. You know what I mean?"

Tim knew, and he thanked the man for his time. No other revelations were found in Woodsfield that day.

The next stop was an afternoon coffee break with Douglas Grant, back in Greenharbor. Tim thought his youthful employer was more tense than usual, and said as much.

"New threats? New notes?"

"Uh...no. Nothing I can pinpoint. Tell me about your research."

"So far, I'd say you've made a bad investment in choosing me. We keep checking backgrounds, looking for that significant something, chasing the lead that will roll the ivory for us."

"Keep going."

Tim took a sip of his limeade. "Doug, regardless of how it makes your uncle look, the best lead we've got is the three-pronged wedge of property that is now owned by one person. We've got to explore that."

Douglas seemed surprised. "You...you think that my uncle..."

"No, don't take it that way. He could be a victim

of circumstances. All I'm saying is...try to visualize some pattern in how that land is changing hands."

"Of course, I'll think about what it could mean. But surely, Tim...that can't be the motive for Sid Burk's death."

"Time will tell." Tim could see that this was not a comfortable subject. "I'll talk with you again the first of the week."

The afternoon was again reaching blast-furnace proportions, and Tim found that Martin was still working on the city audit. Therefore, Tim drove home, parked his car and walked on up the road to Shawn's place. They swam in the shaded pond for an hour.

On Friday, Tim was extremely pleased to welcome Lisa home. When he got her alone in his car, he greeted her with a prolonged kiss.

"The hot weather must be affecting your personality," she teased him.

"Hey. Virgos are great lovers. We just prefer to take our time."

"I wish I had known you were going to be around so much this summer," she told him quite solemnly. "I might have made less involved school plans."

"Ah-h. Get your education. That's more important for you than I am."

"Are you dead sure of that?"

His glance returned to her eyes. "Uh...no. I'm not." He put his arms around her and kissed her a second time.

After having their evening meals at their separate houses, Tim and Lisa met once more. Martin had a date with some secretary he had met at Sumoto's office building. Tim had an invitation to see Mr. Rankin, who had just that day returned to the Greenharbor Motel. He took Lisa along and drove into town.

"Come in, come in," the affable businessman greeted them in his stentorian, fine-toned voice. "Glad you could make it. Sorry I'll only be in town one day, but pressing business keeps me hopping. Listen, folks...oh, sit down, won't you...I made a few calls up Cleveland way, since that seems to be where this Grant pettifogger likes to hang out. Well, I got lucky. Is the man trying to develop a business park hereabouts? You bet he is. Can we prove it? Thanks to a friend in Cleveland who runs a fast copying machine, we sure can. Take a look at this letter, Tim and Lisa. Just look at it!"

Tim unfolded the photocopy of a letter that Rankin handed him. It had been typed on Elston Grant's stationery. The wording, signature and lack of a typist's initials indicated the letter had been composed by Douglas Grant, acting on his uncle's orders. With Lisa looking on, they studied the content.

>Pelco Corporation
>1100 Munsinger road
>Cleveland, Ohio 44102
>
>Dear Mr. Hauser:
>   My uncle has instructed me to write you, to affirm our interest in development studies for an industrial complex, possibly to be in Greenharbor, Ohio. We want to work with you, to determine whether to build a brand new facility, or to expand either of two existing sites.
>   As for the latter possibility, we wish to recommend the newly cleared industrial park zone at Delaware and River streets, designed to stretch southward from the ball park some one-half mile. Equipped with two available buildings and accessible from four city streets, this location has much to commend it.
>   We in Greenharbor are most eager to hear and to consider your thoughts relative to these sites.
>
>Sincerely,
>Douglas Grant
>Legal Assistant to Elston Grant

"It's noteworthy, Mr. Rankin," Tim nodded with a bemused look on his face. "Informative, but not devastating. For one thing, it's Douglas's letter, and for another, it seems to recommend an industrial site within Greenharbor."

"Yes, you're right; that's the first impression. But who's to say that Grant wouldn't pull a shell game, tell them the in-town place was too expensive after all, and shouldn't they consider instead his own property?"

"Well, maybe..."

"You see, Tim, this is a chain of several links. We've now established that Elston Grant is quite interested in property development. Thanks to two murders, he now owns a tidy chunk of soil. Links, my good man. We're forging links."

"Beg your pardon, but isn't this letter over two years old?" asked Lisa as she squinted at the fuzzy date.

"So it is. Pelco never built here. So Grant's still trying. Perhaps he's trying much too hard."

Tim contemplated the matter quietly for several seconds. "Let's pinch our bet, and study this carefully before we confide in the sheriff. Oh, would you mind if I had a copy?"

"There's a machine down the hall. Let's amble that way and try it out."

The three of them explored the growing questions about Elston Grant, but were forced to conclude that there was now a circumstantial case against him. Tim was surprised to learn that Rankin already had heard about the phony rifle sale to Uncle Everett, and marveled anew at how rumor and gossip flew so swiftly in a small community.

"One more thing," Rankin interjected as they paused at his doorway. "My wife will be coming to town with me."

Chapter Fourteen

Proprietary funds are used to account for governmental activities that are conducted in a businesslike fashion, that is, providing goods or services to specific users for a charge that is based on the cost of the activity. The amount of the charge will depend on the operating philosophy of the governmental unit.

Joseph Razek
Gordon A. Hosch

Monday was the twelfth of June, and the week was starting off as warm and humid as the previous week had been. Tim sat in the shade of one of the elm trees in Shawn's front yard, talking with his friend and nursing a wine cooler that Shawn had prepared for him. Martin and Tim had spent eight hours on Saturday watching PADI videos and listening to Shawn explain scuba diving. PADI stood for Professional Association of Diving Instructors.

At noon Martin's dark blue Chrysler convertible rolled to a stop amid the trees of Sparlin Farm. Martin scrambled out of the front seat and hurried over to where his compatriots sat. There was an exuberant smile on his handsome, tanned face. "I've got an announcement."

"This can only mean trouble," Tim told Shawn.

"Truly." Shawn looked up at Martin. "Sorry, I can't vote for you."

"Pay attention, guys. I think I've found the skim at city hall."

"Congratulations."

Martin slid into a lawn chair. "And if *my* problem's solved, I surely hope we won't have to hang around Greenharbor for another five years, just to unravel the murder case."

"I hope not." Tim took another sip of his drink.

"So tell us about your discovery."

"It's a good scheme. I got a random sample of the cash utility payments. Luckily they were computer tapes which indicate the nature of the receipt: cash, check, or credit card. I matched these tapes with the bank deposit slips, and in every instance the total deposit matched the total income for each test."

"So where's the skim?" Shawn asked.

"There's more. The total cash deposited each day was less than recorded on the cash register tape, while the total of checks and credit cards deposited was always in excess of the amount recorded on the register tape."

"So what's your conclusion?" Tim asked.

"Well," Martin smiled, "apparently someone rang up all of the cash amounts correctly as received. But---he or she held back some of the checks and credit cards. When they decided how much cash they wanted to take home for the day, they would remove the cash and substitute a like amount of credit cards and checks. Neat. There was no effect on the total amount deposited."

Tim said, "Let me guess what you did. You calculated the difference between the amount of cash deposited and the cash recorded. This difference is the amount pilfered by the person."

"Right," confirmed Martin. "We have them now!"

Tim and Martin practices swimming with their fins for almost an hour. Tim saw a few small fish and a large turtle as he practiced snorkeling.

* * *

Tim walked to the law office, barely two blocks away at Adams and Massachusetts streets. Douglas met him at the receptionist's desk, and suggested that they talk in the second floor lunchroom.

Doug ordered coffee and Tim had iced tea.

"I've done some careful and serious thinking since our last talk," Doug said as he stirred some sugar into his drink. "The reasoning that tends to lead to a total of eight suspects is sound. I mean, it fits. There's no way to escape it. And, I can agree to cut your uncle and aunt from the list. By the way, did I sound defensive the other day, when you mentioned my uncle?"

"Perhaps. Let's face facts---we've both got an uncle under suspicion. Neither of us is comfortable with that."

"Yes, but...well...the chips have to fall where they happen to fall."

"I take it that you've got something specific in mind."

Douglas had another drink of his coffee, then leaned forward and spoke more softly. "I was talking with Verna Barger yesterday. She just happened to learn that Ling Sumoto made a speech to some Japanese-American businessmen about a year ago. In this speech he urged the group to build a memorial, of sorts, that would emphasize the Japanese contribution to commerce and civic growth in the Midwest. What he seemed to want was a way to combine an industrial park with a memorial, and a research center, and...throw in some restaurants, too.

Not exactly a Japanese Disneyland, but something nice...and something he planned to locate near Greenharbor."

"Sounds like a perfectly reasonable thing to say to a group of Japanese-Americans."

"Maybe he wanted to build it along Route 7. Maybe that's why he was at Orick Farm, trying to buy some land."

"How does that lead to murder? Mr. Sumoto is wealthy and can buy land if he wants land."

"I completely agree that Mr. Sumoto would not have premeditated Burk's death. But Tim---who's to say that Burk's murder was planned in advance? Isn't that just something that you've assumed?"

"Yes...it's an assumption. I base it on the clear evidence that from Burk's death to the present, the killer has been very calculating and two-faced."

"So we need to look for someone who's stoic, unemotional, coldly reserved..."

Tim frowned. "Well, a lack of back-slapping gregariousness does not make one a more likely murderer."

"But did it have to be planned?"

"No. It might have been an argument, of something like that. Give me your scenario."

"Sumoto drives out to see Orick Farm. It borders Route 7 and would be a great start on his Japanese-American industrial park. He has a figure in mind. Mrs. Barger informs him that it's twice that much. He's angered. He storms over to see Sid Burk, and demands to know why the price is higher."

"Pardon my interruption, but Mr. Sumoto told me that he didn't know who actually owned Orick Farm. Mrs. Barger was keeping it quiet."

"Did it occur to you that he might have had reason to lie?"

"Let's suppose he did lie, for the moment. Why kill Sid Burk?"

"It was never meant to happen. They argued, they insulted each other---it got out of hand. In any event, the gun went off, and Burk was dead. I've heard there were bloodstains in Burk's garage. It could've happened there."

"So the cover-up began."

"Yes, and one other point. To put an adult male body in a car trunk would require a lot of strength. Ling isn't that young and isn't that strong. I think he sent for help. That explains why Novia had to claim she was in some great hurry for a check, and dashed out there to a flooded area where she had never gone before, when she could easily have met him in town an hour or so later."

"Then you're suggesting that Ling and Novia put the body in the trunk, and took steps to incriminate my uncle."

"Yes."

"Hmmm." Tim drank some tea. "I don't see why Novia would want to be so helpful in such a dangerous scheme."

"Tim, it's fairly well known in this town that probably half of Novia's paycheck comes out of Sumoto's bank account. Maybe he promised her a raise, and she thought one was long overdue."

Tim finished his tea. "There's a possibility...a slight one... that your right. But how on earth can it be proven?"

"To start with, I'm going to get a copy of that speech he gave."

"It's in print?"

"I've heard that it is. I'll know before the day is over."

"Good. Start there. I'll pursue some of your theory's loose ends, until Friday. Then I'm off with Lisa, headed for a two-day trip down to that old amusement park north of Cortino, in West Virginia."

"I...I'm not sure I know where it is."

"I've only been past it. But Mr. Rankin and three other people are refurbishing it. He invited Lisa and me to take a look at the place."

"Well, have fun. I plan to camp out with some friends, in northern Ohio. It's about time I got away from here for a weekend."

Tim walked with Doug back to the law office, and they made plans to meet again as soon as a copy of the speech could be obtained.

Tim then walked the short distance to the Pasta Superba, where he found Martin sitting at one of the tables.

"How'd it go with Doug?"

Tim dropped into a seat across from Martin. "Well, to sum it up, our friend Doug has developed a theory about Burk's killer. But I don't think you'll like it."

"Try me."

"He thinks Ling Sumoto is the murderer, with a little help from Novia."

"Any proof?"

"We'll both be looking for some, this week."

Martin shook his head. "It sounds to me as though Douglas Grant is getting somewhat desperate to prove his uncle's innocence."

"That thought has crossed my mind. But, while I can

automatically reject Uncle Everett and Aunt Mildred as suspects, I can't escape the fact that the other six have until recently been complete strangers with unknown pasts and unknown motivations. We've got to dig, check alibis, and be careful who we're alone with."

"I'll be careful, Tim---but I'm *not* ready to start being paranoid."

A few moments later, Tim was surprised to feel someone touching his arm.

"Tim."

Lost in thought, Tim was briefly disoriented as he looked up to see Douglas Grant.

"Oh, hi, Doug. Have you eaten?"

"No. Maybe later. Listen, I've got that speech we talked about, and I really need to show it to you."

Tim could tell from the earnest expression on Doug's face that he meant now. At first it was tempting to say "Can't it wait?" But Tim noted that Martin had cut no corners when it came to fulfilling his obligation to Ling Sumoto. In a sense, Tim had the same relationship to Douglas.

"If Martin will excuse me." Tim stood up and left his friend to follow Douglas out of the bustling cafe.

Martin called from the background, "I'll be here when you get back."

They crossed the street and headed for the alley that ran southward from Massachusetts Street. Doug had parked his car at a slight angle in the alley, the passenger-side door being closer to them. He unlocked the door for Tim, then scooted around the rear bumper and slid into the driver's side.

When they were both seated, Doug flashed one of his brief smiles and started the engine. "I wasn't too confident about leaving my car in the alley like this. Figured the city cops might ticket it."

"They know how to write?" Tim fastened his safety belt. "Come on, Doug. Those two old fossils don't even go to the john without asking Kruger for directions."

Douglas Grant turned east onto Massachusetts and then north onto Route 7. "The copy I've got was dropped off at my house."

Three minutes later, Doug turned left into the Grant driveway. "This'll give you some food for thought," he told his passenger.

Tim was about to compare the mental food with the filling meal he had just consumed, when the ugly crack of a rifle sounded.

Doug hit the brake, then let up. "My God, I think he hit the car."

Tim's heart raced. If a gunman was pausing to take

better aim, then either young man could be killed within seconds.

"Stop the car! Get down!" Tim shouted.

Doug jerked his Mercury to a halt in the driveway.

"Could you tell where it hit?" Tim asked.

Both men crouched below windshield level.

"My side. Just above my window. Must have deflected."

"That means he's shooting from the south. We'd better try our luck north."

His seatbelt off, Tim slid out the passenger door.

Doug followed. "Good thinking, Tim."

"Unless there are two of them, covering both sides. In that case, we're about to die."

"Only one guy fired."

"That's true. Look, we can't stay here. How about the house?"

"I don't have any weapons. But we can call the sheriff."

"Is your uncle home?"

"No. He had a meeting."

"Come on. We'll have to circle around, using the few trees we've got, and run for the house. You got a backdoor key?"

"Yeah."

"Then we'll try the back."

It was a panicky exercise, running from tree to tree, uncertain where to stand as a shield to the next bullet, and frightened that a carefully aimed shot could kill either of them. Tim felt sick. From time to time, he glanced at the Grant house. Supposedly a house was a place of safety. But could they be sure that no gunman awaited them in there? If they ran toward another sanctuary, they would continue to make targets of themselves.

It seemed like half an hour, but it was actually two minutes until Douglas and Tim unlocked the back door and dashed into the house. Tim pulled out his pocketknife in case someone was waiting, but the house seemed quiet.

Doug called the sheriff while Tim caught his breath.

Two deputies arrived within minutes, and the entire nightmare began to recede.

Doug pointed out the fresh scrape marks of a bullet, just above the driver's side door. To one of the deputies he asked, "Would I have been any safer if I'd had my glass rolled up?"

"Nope. It's not bulletproof, son."

"Then...then I could've been killed."

"Looks like," said the deputy as he extended a measuring tape, "you escaped death by eight inches."

Chapter Fifteen

The difference between Trust and Agency Fund is one of degree. Trust Funds are sometimes subject to complex administrative and accounting provisions as specified in detailed trust agreements. In addition, Trust Funds may be in existence for a long period of time, and may involve the management and investment of trust assets. The equation for Agency Funds is simply: Assets = Liabilities.
Leonard A. Mikula

Despite a thorough search, no trace of a gunman was found. A spent cartridge turned up, and was tagged for the lab.

Doug apologized for the fourth time about Tim's not getting back to the Pasta Superba.

"Will you knock off the apologies? I'm just glad we survived." Tim touched Doug's shoulder, then slowly pulled his hand back. He felt awkward. In a way he felt closer to Doug, and wanted to reassure him, but the rule remained---don't touch the person who hasn't touched you.

"Thank goodness you were with me." Doug paused a moment, pulling off the tie that his job so often kept him in. Then he stepped over to the window and looked out. "I don't think they'll find a thing."

Tim sat down in one of the comfortable living room chairs. "I'm getting more eager by the minute to find out where each of the five other suspects in Burk's murder may have been tonight."

Doug stopped at the liquor cabinet. "That could pay dividends, maybe. But who's to say that the killer would dare to risk his own neck? Why not hire a marksman?"

"Possible."

Doug opened the cabinet. "What'll it be, Tim?"

"Nothing, thanks."

"We've been through enough that we can have a drink together...I would say."

Tim's mind jumped back to his awkward touch of Doug's shoulder. "You're right. Okay. I'll have a scotch and soda."

Tim stepped forward and accepted the glass. "When this ordeal is all over, we'll probably be old friends."

"I hope so." Doug picked up some stapled papers that were lying on the stereo. "Here's Sumoto's speech."

Tim read the first page carefully. It was given

entirely to introductory remarks and thank yous. The second page was more of the same. Tim's pace slowed as he began the third page. 'All of us would gain from such a complex. It would enhance our heritage. It would pass along values to the next generation. It would show our many contributions to this region and the country. So let us have a tribute of memory, cast in concrete and quickened by the hard work of our generation.'

'Many facets and many structures must be designed and built. To the north, a park and recreation center. To the east, with a stream of beauty, a culture display. To the south, among trees, a selection of places to eat. To the west, on a sloping hill, a research library. Let us give fortune a chance to shine for our posterity.'

"Okay," Tim said, "I think I'm seeing what you're seeing."

* * *

Refreshed after a night's rest, Tim began Tuesday with breakfast and with telling his aunt about the shooting. Uncle Everett was already doing chores. Since only half of his intended audience was there, Tim decided it would be fitting to tell only half the story. So he didn't mention that he was a passenger in the car. Having discharged that duty, Tim and Martin drove the short distance to the Grant property.

"Where might Doug's uncle be today?"

"I'm not sure. Doug said there was a good chance he'd be away overnight. He's a traveling attorney, you know."

"Yeah. Where was he in time and space at the very moment you two were being shot at?"

"I'm not sure. What's your supposition---that Elston Grant might go so far as to warn off his nephew with a rifle bullet?"

"Well said. In trusting his uncle's innocence so fully, Doug could be flying on the wings of failure."

"I agree with you, Martin. In fact, why don't you and Sheriff Kruger see if you can pinpoint what the five other members of the group of eight were doing? That could keep you busy this weekend while Lisa and I get a little time off."

"Don't forget to keep an eye on Rankin. While you're at it, ask *him* what he was doing yesterday."

"A marvelous idea." Tim wiped some sweat from his forehead, noting that it was already starting to be a muggy day. "For some strange reason, I'm beginning to feel like I'm in a game of madhouse poker, and the stakes are being raised every two or three days."

"With bullets for chips."

The young men spent twenty minutes prowling through the trees in search of missed clues, but none turned up. The high humidity made matters worse. At length, Martin leaned against a tree and folded his arms. "You know something? I think I'd like Shawn even if he didn't have a clean, shady pond. But with it, I'm absolutely crazy about visiting him."

"I second the motion."

* * *

Tim and Martin had passed the written scuba diving exam the previous Saturday. Today was the open water diving test.

Shawn took Tim and Martin 30 feet down in the pond, where the bottom was sandy. Tim and Martin ran through smoothly a number of underwater tests, such as achieving neutral buoyancy, taking off their masks and then putting them on and blowing out the water, and buddy breathing. The earlier practice sessions paid off. Tim only had trouble taking off the air tank, regulator and buoyancy compensator and then putting them back on at the bottom of the pond. The task was similar to putting on a jacket and backpack while driving 55 miles per hour on a narrow road.

After finishing all of the tests, Shawn pointed to what appeared to be an underwater cave as they were ascending to the surface.

On the surface, Tim asked Shawn about the dark cave.

Shawn siad, "We'll go through the cave when you two both improve. It's fairly large, but it goes to the river."

"To the river!" Tim almost shouted. "Do you mean that someone could get here by diving from the river, through the cave, into the pond?"

"Sure, if he or she was an expert diver," Shawn answered.

"So there could be more than six suspects," Tim shouted.

"Whoa," said Shawn. "I know what you're suggesting. The river was extremely rough. It was overflowing its banks during the murder. It would have taken a Navy seal."

"Still, I wonder," Tim replied.

Tim, Martin and Shawn reluctantly left their reinvigorating pond and their diving lesson at three thirty on Friday afternoon. Shawn was headed for a music rehearsal, and after that planned to join Martin at the Pasta Superba. Tim had to telephone Douglas

Grant before picking up Lisa and meeting the Rankins.

"I hope you two enjoy your weekend. Lisa and I will be thinking about you...when our minds aren't on other subjects."

Martin cleared his throat. "Remember, Tim, keep your eyes *on* Rankin and your hands *off* Lisa."

"And don't get those orders turned around," Shawn added.

Ten minutes later, Tim and Martin stopped at the Whinney house and telephoned Douglas at his Greenharbor office. He informed them that he would stop briefly at his house for some camping gear and hiking clothes.

Since he was being accompanied by a deputy, Douglas insisted that Tim begin his weekend without stopping at the Grant property. "This weekend ought to provide a breather for both of us," the young paralegal said.

Tim hung up the phone. "Well, that's that. You'd better go count some more customers. I'm taking my best girl on a short summer holiday, and I guarantee you that we'll enjoy ourselves."

"Just watch yourself, Tim. We still don't know beans about Rankin. He could turn out to be something less than the charming old soul he claims to be."

"It's just a pleasant little weekend jaunt, Martin. What could possibly go wrong?"

Chapter Sixteen

The expense of government to the individuals of a great nation is like the expense of management of the joint tenants of a great estate, who are obliged to contribute in proportion to their respective interests in the estate. In the observation of neglect of this maxim consists, what is called the equality or inequality of taxation.
                              Adam Smith

   Tim drove Lisa to the Greenharbor Motel, where they were greeted by a congenial middle-aged lady, slim and dapperly dressed in a violet skirt and blouse. She introduced herself as Grace Rankin.
   "You're Tim Whinney, and you're Lisa Flinn. It's such a pleasure to meet you. Come in before you melt in this fiery heat."
   Inside, Walter Rankin was just closing a suitcase.
   "Hello, there, Tim and Lisa! I see you've met my better half."
   Within minutes, the four of them had Mr. Rankin's Oldsmobile Ninety-Eight loaded and on the road. The two couples had no difficulty in keeping a conversation going. Tim discovered that Mr. Rankin liked model railroading and Mrs. Rankin did some local theater and wrote poems.
   "Everybody's got something that he or she really wants to do, but never quite jumps into," Mr. Rankin theorized as he passed a truck. "Now, take me. Would any of you believe that I've always fancied myself as a top-drawer private detective? I'm somewhat of a Sherlock Holmes nut. I hope to build myself a Holmes' world wide web page, but there's so many out there now."
   The silence was deafening. Finally, Tim acquiesced.
 "I'm sure anybody could be a sleuth, with the proper incentive. Most of us have no compelling reason to investigate a crime, and we know the police are better trained than we are. But I've always been amazed with Holmes' deductive reasoning ability."
   "True, true. But sometimes a clever and astute individual can make a towering contribution. Which reminds me, Tim...how is your own investigation doing?"
   "Well, it's..." He paused for several seconds, considering a plethora of possible answers. "It's tightening up, to be quite honest. Douglas Grant is eliminated, unless of course he hired someone to take a shot at the car we were in."
   Tim was surprised by the startled expressions that

greeted his statement. Only then did he fully realize that none of the other three knew of the shooting. The cannonade of questions that followed made it equally clear that each of the trio was thirsty for details.

Tim explained the situation as best he remembered it. "Gosh, I was sure the local press or radio station would've filled the air with barnburning prose."

"In *Greenharbor*? It takes them three days to write the copy," Lisa said.

"Why don't we stop in New Matamoras for supper?" Mr. Rankin suggested. "We can give this shooting business a proper airing. In fact, we might've been smarter to have stayed in Greenharbor this weekend, and tried to locate this killer."

Tim caught Lisa's glance and realized she was in no mood for a hasty retreat to Greenharbor.

"I think that would be pointless, Mr. Rankin. Doug's away for the weekend, the area by his house has been combed and recombed, and once again the next move is up to the murderer. Maybe getting some distance from Greenharbor, and some perspective on our options, is precisely what we need."

"Sounds wise to me," Grace Rankin said. "Besides, I want to see this amusement park."

Dinner in New Matamoras took less than an hour. The conversation about who might have tried to shoot Douglas Grant, and why, and whether he or she meant to miss and whether a hired rifleman might have been employed, ultimately meandered to the same uncertain conclusions that Tim and Martin had reached. Tim mentioned the fact that there was an underwater cave from Shawn's pond to the river, but no one believed that such a cave would expand the suspect list.

Perhaps the only significant difference was that this discussion of rifles and victims and evil motives was conducted at an open table, where it drew the attention of at least one busybody eating nearby. As the foursome headed back to their car, the elderly patron could not constrain herself from asking, "Are you folks writing a play?"

"No," replied Grace Rankin without batting an eyelash. "We're munitions experts for the C.I.A."

Outside, Tim told Grace that C.I.A. also stood for Certified Internal Auditors. "They have an excellent internal auditing program at Louisiana State University." Grace laughed.

They crossed the Ohio River near the north edge of Newport, via the Carpenter Bridge, and headed southwest on West Virginia Route 2. Cortino was a short distance away, so it became obvious that there would be plenty of daylight to tour the amusement park.

One mile north of Cortino, Mr. Rankin signaled a left turn and passed through a rusty iron arch. As they crunched along on a gravel roadbed, a homemade sign gave them the name of their surroundings as Mil-Star Amusement Park. The roadway widened, and Rankin rolled to a stop near a huge tent.

"You may need a map to avoid getting lost," the host told his entourage. "We've got some inside the main tent here. I want all of you to meet O'Dell."

Tim and Lisa both pocketed smaller photocopied versions of the large map that hung on an improvised wooden wall in the gigantic tent that was designed like a park shelter. Mil-Star encompassed over twenty acres, with room near the southeast corner for even more expansion. Despite the immensity of the land area, only three small teams of workers were laboring on various rides and landscaping projects. Accordingly, unfinished structures were everywhere, and it seemed as if a great deal of time would pass before the public could be entertained there. "O'Dell! Come over a minute, will you? I want you to meet my wife and two friends of ours. Maybe give them a tour."

A wizened man some five inches shorter than Tim strode over to the group. Despite his slight limp and wrinkled face, O'Dell seemed to be a man full of energy and enthusiasm. He greeted everyone with a firm handshake. In answer to Grace Rankin's query, he assured the group that relatives, friends, strangers, and bill collectors all called him O'Dell, as he had forgotten any other names he might once have had.

"Not even *Mr.* O'Dell?" Lisa asked.

"Especially not that. Can't stand titles and stuffy formality. O'Dell's the handle that lifts the pot."

There was a touch of Irish lilt to his speech.

"We gather that you've been here from the very beginning," Tim suggested.

"Indeed so. Been sittin' on this green little run for twenty years, hopin' and prayin' that we'd crank her up some day. If I'd had the money, I'd have put this place in shape *long* ago. It's a dream come true, I tell ya, to see this equipment rollin' in here, and more rails bein' laid. Let's take a look at it!"

O'Dell led his party of four underneath a flapping canvas overhang, and steered them southward along a wide walking lane. The temperature and humidity had both dropped, even as the western sun had started to touch the tall surrounding hills. A few idle clouds, promising but not bringing rain, favored the group with a lessening of the summer glare.

"Rides'll be here," O'Dell announced. "Both sides of this street." At present there were concrete foundations only.

"So you've sat on this land, pastoring it for years and years," Grace said. "I understand you've worked long and thankless hours to find investors."

"Yes ma'am," returned O'Dell without bitterness. "At times I thought I'd not live to see it. But things turned around."

"You went the whole pile, and now there's heavy sugar," Tim observed.

"Card talk," O'Dell noted dryly.

"Oh, look at that!" Lisa exclaimed as she pointed toward a tall bronze statue near the crossroads ahead.

"Hermes, the god of fairs," explained O'Dell. "I bought that for a song, many a year ago. Ain't he a novelty? Hermes was a messenger, and always in a hurry. Guess he never had time to bother with clothes."

"Was this land ever used for a county fair?"

"Indeed it was, Miz Rankin, long and far ago. But the townsfolk got uppity and moved the whole works to a pasture on the other side of Cortino."

They walked on past Hermes, and began to see some assembled rides. A merry-go-round and a set of vampire jets were the first.

"Tell them about the name," urged Walter Rankin.

"Perhaps they can guess. What would you think Mil-Star might mean?"

"A million stars," surmised Grace.

"The Milky Way," Lisa guessed.

"Perhaps Mr. Miller and Mr. Stark," was Tim's contribution.

O'Dell stopped walking and shook his head. "You should spend more time readin' history and less time playin' cards, young man. This park is named after two of the most famous fair centers of the Middle Ages---Milan and Stourbridge. Tradin' fairs were the lifeblood of the old order---their Wall Street and Knowledge Exchange, all rolled into one. Stourbridge, Champagne, Leipzig and Milan were four of the big centers. From those serious beginnings we worked our way down to the amusement park of today. A change for the worse, many would say, but I'm not one to raise my voice against a little fun."

Except for card playing, Tim thought to himself, but he kept quiet.

They walked on, past signs indicating that a scrambler and an octopus would soon appear at those spots. Then O'Dell turned left and led the group eastward, canting past some trees and brush with the

Appalachian foothills not far in the distance. We're comin' to it now," O'Dell said with a note of triumph in his voice. He brushed an unruly lock of white hair away from his forehead.

Tim and Lisa were bringing up the rear. He put his arm around her shoulder.

"Having a fun hike?"

"It's different. We ought to come back when it opens."

"It'll only be fun for couples. Going to someplace like this alone makes you feel like the whole world has deserted you."

"*There* it is," O'Dell proclaimed with a sweeping gesture of his left arm.

They looked up to see gigantic trestles spiraling into the air, holding up a wooden track that arched more than a hundred feet over their heads.

"Our pride and joy," O'Dell beamed. "A wooden roller coaster fit for a king. Old Froggy Thurston would be *proud* of this un'."

Tim tilted his head back and looked almost straight up as the sun again darkened. The wood and steel structure had the appearance of an old railroad---an ancient railroad, perhaps, now decrepit and forlorn. A wisp of breeze came by, momentarily chilling the warm air and causing a few loose boards to clatter with a hollow, desolate sound. The nearby brush was coated with a rusty film that seemed to have dripped down from the imposing structure high above.

"Is this old track safe?" Tim asked.

"Needs a lot of repair," O'Dell replied. "Some of the rail is rusty, and the timber rots the most where the ride track stays in contact with damp soil---the valley points, as some folk call 'em."

"I've always wondered what powers these things," Grace said. "Does the lead car or engine run on electricity?"

"No ma'am. It's a gravity ride. An elevator device pulls the train to the top of the rail---the startin' position. The momentum the coaster picks up as it sails down that first incline is what gives it the initial thrust. From then on, it's on its own. We've been clever about this, takin' full advantage of the foothills already here."

Mr. Rankin rubbed his chin. "I got word on the phone yesterday that the four-car coaster was in place, and your workers were testing the lift that pulls them up to the starter peak. Is that wise? This old track can't handle a coaster yet, can it?"

"Oh, as it stands, sir, we've got brakes to stop the

cars, and we don't go beyond the second zenith. We've got to check some track width, and usin' the coaster is the best way I know to do it. We keep it a far piece away from the old rotten trackbed near the waterspill."

"That's best, I'm sure."

"What was that article you were showing me on Wednesday?" Grace Rankin appeared bored with the discussion. "About roller coasters."

"The track that came apart in New York. Killed twenty people," Mr. Rankin answered.

"That's right," said Grace. "The article said the heavily-hyped thrill rides at many theme parks are often work-in-progress."

"Work-in-process?" Tim asked.

"No, they said work-in-progress," Grace answered. "When new rides are built, the industry expects injuries. They gave an example of the terrifying Timber Wolf ride in Kansas City. On its opening day in 1990, a complete malfunction, and one of the trains smacked into the back of another one—48 people hurt."

Grace paused. "The article said that the first year of a new ride is a trial year. The theme park makes enough corrections and adjustments to eliminate most of the injuries."

"Trial and error," Tim repeated. "Work-in-progress. Those sound like accounting terms."

"Six Flags, Houston's AstroWorld, and the Fiesta Texas theme parks have revamped their wildest amusement rides to reduce injuries and lawsuits," Grace continued.

Lisa swallowed hard. "Do you suppose we could wander on our way, and get some distance between us and this spooky old bridge? I don't want to be a guinea pig."

"I suppose we could," O'Dell said as he stepped back on the gravel pathway. "Let me show you the shootin' gallery and dinin' tent."

Lisa glanced at Tim, a frown on her face. "*Twenty* people?"

"I've read that people feel they're twice rewarded by amusement park rides. Once because of the entertainment, and secondly because they've cheated death," Mr. Rankin suggested.

As Lisa stepped away, the sun popped out and cast a zebra shadow on the jagged seam of exposed rock that lay just east of the trestlework. Tim took one last look up at the ominous, hoary structure. "A wee bit creepy," he mumbled.

"We're talking about controlled terror," Mr. Rankin smiled.

Forty minutes later, the Rankins and their two

guests had checked in at the Cortino Motel, some two miles southwest of the amusement park. The middle-aged couple had plans to see a movie, and invited Tim and Lisa along to the town's only cinema.

"Thanks anyway," Tim smiled, "but it's been a long day, and I'm planning to turn in early."

"And...I have some reading for my taxation course to do," Lisa added.

"Then we'll see you both for breakfast tomorrow, as planned," Grace said brightly as she stepped toward the lobby's front door. Show time was approaching, and they needed to hurry along.

"Well-l," Tim said a few moments later, "it seems as though we are alone at last."

"Finally."

"Time for us to get started on our thoroughly respectable and totally separate evening plans."

Lisa put her hands together. "I don't know about you, but I can get my reading assignment out of the way in thirty seconds flat."

"College work isn't what it used to be."

With her fingers she began to play with the lowest button on his shirt. "I'll tell you what. Give me about thirty minutes to shower and put myself together, and I'll drop by for a visit," she promised.

"I'll be home. Room 145."

* * *

Twenty minutes later, Tim had kicked off his shoes and unbuttoned his shirt. His room was pleasantly cool, and he decided to stretch out on his bed. To kill a few minutes and to keep himself awake, he turned on the television. Under the circumstances, he was surprised to find himself yawning, but it had in fact been a long, hot day. He closed his eyes. As soon as Lisa got there, the night would come alive.

Outside the door, a dark-clad figure tried the doorknob and found it unlocked. Cautiously, the door was opened. Stealthy steps brought the intruder closer to the bed. A small towel came into view, and a strong-smelling liquid was poured on the towel.

With the quickness of a striking cobra, the black figure leaped atop Tim, forcing the towel against the young man's nose and mouth. For a few moments the struggle was furious, but the element of surprise proved critical.

A minute later, Tim lay on the bed unconscious. A needle went into his arm, and the attacker prevailed over the prey.

Chapter Seventeen

For governmental funds, fund equity is the excess of net fund assets over fund liabilities. Fund equity in proprietary funds, however, is the net total assets over total liabilities. The essential difference between the two is fund versus total assets and liabilities, caused by the differences in the measurement focus of the two primary fund types.

Rhett D. Harrell

Lisa found no one in Tim's unlocked room. As the minutes passed, she became increasingly concerned. When she decided that there were no longer any rational explanations, she picked up the room phone and contacted the front desk.

"I'm in Room 145. I want to speak to the manager. Immediately. And I also need someone paged at a local theater."

Lisa's anguished grimness tended to pour cold water on empty reassurances that nothing was really wrong.

When Mr. and Mrs. Rankin arrived, along with a deputy sheriff, they all seemed to sense that something was very wrong.

"Tim is missing. He was waiting for me to come up and talk about my research paper. When I got here, the door was unlocked and he was gone. Not his shoes, just Tim. That was eight thirty-five. It's now a quarter 'til ten. There's no word from him."

Mr. Rankin immediately comprehended that Lisa was deeply worried, and had cause to be. His eyes darted from her to the motel manager. "Could he have fallen ill in one of the restrooms? You have public restrooms here, don't you?"

"Uh...yes...we've done some checking."

The deputy sheriff cleared his throat. "I suggest that all of us take a quick look around. Bathrooms, outside shrubs...anyplace a sick person might have collapsed. I'll call the hospital and see what they know. Let's meet back here in ten minutes." The searchers began to disperse, leaving the deputy and Lisa alone in Tim's room.

"Begging your pardon, ma'am, but is there any chance the two of you had a little quarrel?"

"We did *not* have a quarrel. He was waiting for me to come up here, but...he was gone."

"All right. I'll call the hospital."

Fifteen minutes later, it was clear that Tim was not lying in plain sight at some spot where a seriously ill person might have stumbled and fallen.

"I think he was put on a cart and wheeled out of here," Lisa theorized.

"That's a bit dramatic." The deputy was down on his knees. "I can't see much of anything here. No impression in the carpet...no cart tracks."

Rankin appeared with a magnifying glass in his hand. "I can. One set, starting here...and going to the door."

"Goodness, Walter, you're beginning to look like Sherlock Holmes with that magnifying glass." Mrs. Rankin was pursuing her own discreet check for drops of blood, but she found none.

The deputy turned to the manager. "Any room service sent up here recently? Any linen deliveries?"

"I don't know. But I can check."

"Let's both check. I'll get the measurements of the carts your workers use."

The two men exited, leaving the Rankins with Lisa.

Walter Rankin sat down uneasily on the edge of the bed.

"I don't like this one iota. His uncle was framed for murder, either he or young Grant was shot at this week, and now this. It's worrisome."

"He could be dead," Lisa said in her most serious voice. "He *could* be dead."

Grace Rankin put a comforting arm around her. "At this point, kidnapping is much more likely. Let's hope for the best."

"Maybe we were followed...all the way from Greenharbor," mused Rankin. "If so, and there are other possibilities, but...anyone following us would've pulled into the amusement park grounds. Hmmm. I'll call out there and see if anyone noticed a car behind us."

Rankin picked up the room phone and obtained an outside line. He dialed the security shack at the amusement park.

"Hmm. Odd. No answer."

"The guard might be on rounds."

"Then someone should be there to watch the front entrance, and cover the phone. O'Dell is very fussy about that. Demands that the car traffic be watched carefully. Afraid of tools being sneaked out."

Rankin hung up, then dialed again. No one answered. "Odd. Quite odd."

The two women turned to face each other.

"You don't suppose..."

"It would be a place..." Grace put one hand on her chin, "...a good place to keep someone...maybe this person explored the park while we were there, thinking about a hiding spot. Walter, I have the strangest feeling that Tim could be at that park."

"Just because the guard doesn't answer? Could be his nap time, you know," Walter suggested.

Lisa brightened a little. "Oh *please* let's go out there. Anything would be better than staying here with no word, staring at these walls...staring at his shoes..."

Grace looked at her husband.

"Well if nothing else," he reasoned, "we might solve the question of why the guard doesn't answer. I need to put on some old clothes. Let's meet at the lobby in about six or seven minutes."

Lisa hurried to her room where she put on low-heeled walking shoes, faded jeans, and an old dark green jacket. Two minutes later she met the Rankins. They were dressed for outdoor work, and each carried a small sack of emergency supplies.

"Let's pull our freight out." Rankin breezed past the deputy, who was standing at the front desk.

"Here...call me at this number if you learn anything. We're headed for the Mil-Star Amusement Park."

The deputy waited until the three searchers had left before he turned to the night clerk. "Guess they're not so worried about that professor after all, if they're all goin' to an amusement park."

Inside their sedan, Mr. Rankin unlocked a small tackle box and removed a revolver, which he loaded.

"We're not dealing with harmless people," was his only comment.

The Oldsmobile made quick work of covering the distance to Mil-Star. They stopped at the gate near the highway and found it locked. But Rankin had a key. In less than a hundred feet they stopped at the small guard shack that stood directly north of the main tent where they had started their afternoon; for Lisa, it was now as bleak as a graveyard at midnight. She remembered his words: "Going to someplace like this alone makes you feel like the whole world has deserted you."

"No sign of that guard," Rankin called out from the shack.

Lisa directed her attention to the graveled street that led southward to the rides and booths. It had been exhilarating to walk with Tim and soak it all in. Oh how quickly the Fates can turn on you, she thought to herself. Like a pagan sacrifice, she felt as if her heart had been sliced out of her body. She paused a moment in the windy gloom, thinking about twenty roller coaster victims, Sid Burk's bullet, Molly Burk's poison, a knifing in the morning paper, and a speech she heard last week demanding electrocution for all violent offenders. "The spirit of murder is abroad in this land," she whispered, perhaps to herself, perhaps to nobody. "He could so easily be dead. Maybe we'll never even find the body." A tear ran down her right cheek. "You should've stayed in Indiana, Tim. And I should die an old maid."

"Lisa!" Grace Rankin approached. "Please don't get separated from us. This place is so dark. Stay right here, and I'll have Walter turn on some of the outside lights."

Grace went away, and Lisa found herself moving aimlessly along the wide pathway. She felt gloomy, rueful, hurt. Something warm and tender and rapturous had been defiled with grime and blood. She wandered on, too sorrow stricken to care about her destination.

Suddenly, she heard a humming and banging sound in the distance. It was so out-of-place that she whirled and looked behind her, startled by its bizarreness.

"Great flying swordfish!" Rankin yelled in the distance. "Some fool has started up the roller coaster!"

"That's it!" Lisa told herself with inexplicable certainty. It all made sense. That threatening, creaky, evil wooden monster. Even Tim found it malefic, and so had the sinister ghost who had followed them to Cortino. Of course! Probably posing as a worker, he---or she---had tagged along on O'Dell's tour. The murderer had shadowed them, and had seen the brooding old trestles, the sagging wood, the murky pools of rusty, oily water by the tracks. Rankin had a booming voice. Had the killer heard Rankin say a roller coaster had killed twenty people? Like a reptilian egg, the idea had hatched---capture Tim, and let the roller coaster kill him. That was it! That's why the guard was out of commission. Logic be hanged---for one brief, terrifying moment, she had locked into the murderer's mind.

"Mr. Rankin! Mrs. Rankin!" Operating on instinct and adrenaline, she felt herself running back toward the guard shack. "Call the police! The sheriff! Get help! Look for the guard---he might still be alive. Tim's somewhere along the roller coaster track. I know it! I'm going to try to save him!" She spun around and dashed southward as fast as she could run.

Grace literally grabbed for her, but captured nothing but an armful of air. "Oh no, Lisa! Come back!"

Walter Rankin shoved the revolver firmly into a hip pocket. "Use the phone, Grace. Get reinforcements. I'm going after her."

Her heart pounding, Lisa raced through the ebony darkness, noticing that wisps of fog were beginning to form. As if any more murkiness was needed. Then, to her right, she saw a landmark. Hermes! A small footlight brought the naked messenger god to life. His bronze arm pointed to the left, and she noticed that a bypath leading to the roller coaster track had been cut through the construction area. They had not gone this route earlier, but Lisa knew she had to cut eastward.

She paused a moment in the silver silence of a half-constructed ride. Gravel was crunching behind her. After easing into a pitch-black crevice, she turned to look to her right.

Rankin was visible in the moonlight, his revolver in his right hand. If he was searching for her, it seemed unusual that he didn't call her name. He stopped at the path crossing, then hurried on southward, away from Lisa's hiding place.

More lights came on, above in the treetops and more to the north. At the same time, there were metallic noises coming from the starting slope of the roller coaster track.

Lisa ran toward the old track, wishing for all the world that she had a flashlight. To her relief, the high lampposts near the trackbed were coming to life.

The footpath forked, and Lisa veered to the south, toward a trio of tall lights and toward a point where the tracks came all the way down to ground level. She recalled something being said about the wood ties being completely rotten at the bottom of each hill---and therefore it was the most likely place to fake an accident. If no one was there, she could at least get on the track at ground level.

Within one second, two jarring sensations flooded her mind. Her ears caught the rumble and rattle of the roller coaster cars beginning their descent. But more frightening was what her eyes saw---a figure beneath the lowest point of the track. It was a human figure with dark legs and a whitish shirt flapping a little in the breeze.

"Tim!" she screamed. The old movie *Roller Coaster* flashed into her mind.

The coaster made less noise as it slowed for the top of the second hill. Lisa ran as fast as she could, reaching Tim's body as the coaster began to clatter more loudly. It was roaring down the second hill.

Tim wasn't moving. His outstretched arms and head

were in a small pool of oily mud, but his nose was free. The unbuttoned light blue shirt was the same one he had worn earlier. She began to tug on his arms in an attempt to extricate his legs from under the steel rails, when she saw to her horror that his legs had been tied to those rails. When the heavy coaster cars passed over the railing, driving it deep into the rotting wood and mud, thousands of pounds would hammer his legs, breaking them or severing them.

She whirled to see how close the roller coaster was, and gasped to find Walter Rankin had just run up behind her.

"Lisa..."

"His *legs*!" she screamed. "He's tied to the rail!"

Rankin pocketed his gun and grabbed a heavy piece of wood. "Maybe I can dislodge it---knock the confounded cars off the track!"

"No!" Lisa shouted, although he went ahead with his plan, running northward to intercept the coaster sooner. Lisa knew that the wheels were designed to prevent track jumping. Rankin and his clumsy club would be useless. Panicky, with only moments to spare, she prayed for a knife.

"Tim's pocketknife!" She thrust her hand into his left front pocket, and pulled out his small knife, somehow getting the blade to open despite her shaking hands. She cut frantically at the ropes, wondering if she would be strong enough to move him even if the bonds were slack.

As she slashed, a dozen thoughts seemed to roar through her head, crazily keeping time with the approaching roller coaster. She knew about the knife because he had pulled it out of his pocket the first time they ever met, at the feed store. He said that he always carried it. Once he told her that in his Indiana junior high school, the boys had been threatened first with detentions and then with beatings if they carried pocketknives. But Tim had been as stubborn as the administrators, and he kept carrying his knife. Now, it just might save his life.

Like a Stygian demon plunging into hell, the huge roller coaster clamored down the third and final grade before reaching Tim. Rankin threw his post, and it did in fact strike the right front wheel, but no dislodging took place. The wood was knocked to one side by the powerful steel wheels, almost hitting Rankin.

Lisa cut through the final rope and tossed the knife behind her. She grabbed Tim's limp arms and pulled with all her might. Every muscle in her body seemed to ache. The coaster was so close that its vibration shook the track, allowing Tim's legs to slide under the metal. His feet were barely six inches clear of the track when the roller coaster flew past. The rail seemed to sink a foot into the mud and rotten ties. Lisa had a mental vision of two legs shattered beyond repair as she felt herself falling backwards. She tried to keep her balance but failed, letting go of Tim and tumbling backwards. Lisa was so exhausted she could hardly move. Her first clear thought was a recognition that Rankin was taking Tim's pulse.

"He's alive. Firm heartbeat."

A deputy sheriff popped up out of nowhere. "We found the guard. Tied up but okay." The deputy put his hand on Lisa's shoulder and turned her to face him. "My apologies, young lady. Guess I'll have to admit that you two didn't have a quarrel."

That Friday night, according to their plan, was to have been the night---fireworks, roses and champagne, all rolled up into one modest motel room. Instead, Tim was taken to the hospital, to spend his night there. He had met Mr. Midnight and won.

* * *

When she went to see him at the hospital at eleven the next morning, Lisa was not one ounce happier. Yes, he was alive. But their weekend---disaster was too kind a word for it.

"Hello, beautiful," Tim said as he took her hand. "I understand that you saved my legs."

"Yes, but I didn't save our weekend."

"We make a good team, Lisa. You save lives; I save weekends."

"What do you mean?"

"I talked to Rankin ten minutes ago. Told him the drug or whatever they put in me would need another day to wear off. Told him a car trip to Greenharbor would make me sick as a dog. We've got to stay over; I insisted, preferably as unregistered guests in more secure rooms."

"You mean...they're letting you out of the hospital?"

"Right. And Mr. Rankin wanted to go sailing back to Greenharbor. That's why I said, 'Hey, no car travel for me.' But don't worry." He winked at her. "I'll start recovering rapidly at nine p.m."

"We get our night?"

"We'll get our night."

114

Chapter Eighteen

Taxes are compulsory payments which individual citizens make, directly and indirectly, for services provided by the government.
                    Dan Troop Smith

   Monday found Tim having breakfast in bed at the Whinney farmhouse. To speed his recovery, he had accepted the medical advice of trying to stay off his feet for two or three days.
   "A delicious breakfast pizza, Martin," Tim said as he laid the plate on his bedside table.
   "I'm glad you liked it. Tim, we're going to have to get moving on this murder case. By my count we had two close misses in a week. And from what I've heard, if Lisa hadn't pulled you out of there, before the weight of that coaster would've passed over your body, you might not've had two legs."
   Tim's smile evaporated. "I guess that's right. I owe her the world, Martin. Maybe I should say that I owe her my life. That's pretty much the truth. I would've bled to death, more than likely."
   "So what's your plan---move on to another university and leave her sitting here, waiting for the farm boy two fields over to propose to her?" He picked up the dish and the silverware.
   "You raise a good point," Tim said. "I used to tell myself that Lisa would never move away from here. Now I'm not so sure, and that brings other questions into focus. Do we really want a life together? Or is this a fleeting summer love? How about you, Martin...you ever come close to getting married?"
   "Yeah. I was engaged for two weeks."
   "What stopped it?"
   "I found out she'd already been divorced twice. Twenty years old, and divorced twice. I backed away. She took offense. It was all over with impressive speed, Tim."
   "Believe it or not, that's what I fear most. That it would cool off, that we'd start hurting each other, and then...nothing to keep you warm at night but a divorce decree."
   Martin shrugged. "It's your decision, old buddy."
   An hour later, Tim and Martin discussed what if anything Tim could recall about his attack.
   "Something went over my face...I was struggling to breathe, then nothing."
   "You didn't wake up until Lisa pulled you out from

under the rails?"

"Barely then. The doctor said I had something in my system like an anesthetic...and they found a needle mark on my arm."

"Tell me what you can. Male or female?"

"I didn't see or hear a thing. Of course I'd like to say that it couldn't have been a woman...that I could've fought her off. But I had only seconds, and I started out half asleep."

"Two people. Would that work?"

"Could've been five. Could've been an initiation into a secret cult, for all I can remember. Sorry."

"Listen, we've got to come up with a better strategy than simply waiting for this murderous creep to strike again."

"You can worry less if you keep busy pursuing the few leads we have. Speaking of which---who was free to shoot at Doug and me last week?"

"Any of five people. None of them has an alibi that couldn't have been faked or bribed. I plan to see how the five remaining suspects spent their weekends."

"Certainly you should do that. But don't forget that it could've been contracted. What we really need---is a breakthrough."

"If I mix the right ingredients, maybe I can pull one of those out of my detective hat."

* * *

On Thursday, Tim felt well enough to drive into Greenharbor. His first stop was Elston Grant's office. It was four p. m. and Grant was still in court, but his efficient secretary---Thelma to almost everyone---was at her desk. She told Douglas of Tim's arrival.

"Tim! Good to see you!" Douglas shook his hand. "Word travels fast in a small town, and I heard that you...uh...had an accident."

"I think somebody tried to kill me." Tim looked closely at Douglas. "And you? No more rifle shots? No warning notes?"

The young paralegal shook his head. "I'm fine. I admit that it made me feel safer to visit my friends quite a bit. Uncle Elston practically has the house to himself, but he seems to resist intimidation of any sort. And, so far, he tells me that no one has tried to threaten him."

"Don't you worry about him?"

"Of course. I mean...I'm still scared. But try to motivate my uncle. Just try. It's...oh...like you'd try to talk a smoker out of smoking. Ever try that?"

"I certainly have. With no results."

Doug's eyes, a darker blue than Tim's, seemed misty for a moment. "Then you know about brick walls. The blood one gets on one's head, from pounding those walls..."

"Your illustrations never stray too far from reality, do they? As best I know, you don't smoke, but your uncle does."

Doug smiled. "Only a pipe and he's cutting down. Say...I've been worried about you. Are you all right?"

"Yes."

"Tell me the truth. I mean...we've managed to be honest with each other, about most things. I've admitted that this...this terrorization has scared me. What about you? Are you scared...I mean...a little, even?"

"Doug, my uncle in Indiana once told me something that I've never forgot. He said, 'If you want to be a knight, the steel that counts isn't in your armor, it's in your character.' Maybe it was my age---I was thirteen then, and impressionable---but I took his words to heart. I decided that from that day on, nobody would intimidate me. Strangely enough, showing a little courage can gain you some ground. When people push me, I've found a way to push back, though not always with force."

"Then it would appear that I made a good choice when I hired you and Martin. The prince and the paladin, destined to conquer and anointed to reign."

Tim laughed. "You overstate it. Perhaps I led you to that precipice. Maybe we should temper all of this nobility with another old maxim: 'From the seed of caution grows the tree of longevity.'"

"Not bad. Words from another wise uncle?"

Tim stood up. "I think that I found that one in a fortune cookie. I'm keeping you from your work. I'd better hit the road."

"Hold on, Tim." Douglas reached for his checkbook and wrote his employee a check for two hundred dollars.

"Keep working and keep me posted. The life you save could be mine, or yours, or somebody's uncle."

"Thanks. I'll get back to work."

Tim drove to the Pasta Superba and walked inside, hoping to find Martin and Shawn there. The plan was partially successful, in that Shawn was sitting at a table by himself.

"Hi. Is Martin around?"

Shawn pointed toward the kitchen. "He rushed into the cooking area about a minute ago. Doreen, the assistant manager, was startled by something, and let out quite a scream."

"Hmmm. I'd better check into this." Tim stepped toward the kitchen and met up with Martin and Doreen at the same time a deputy sheriff arrived. Doreen seemed pale, and had evidently been upset by something.

"Got a report of some trouble here," the deputy said.

"I'm okay now," Doreen said, sounding as if she wasn't. "It's over here by the oven." She led while Tim, Martin and the deputy followed. "It's just that...for one horrible second...I thought it was a human head."

Everyone looked at the cutting table. In the middle of it was an overly brown pizza and a large glob of cream-colored plastic. It was easy enough to tell that the plastic had until recently been a mannequin's head. Taped to the oven door was a typed note. The note, bearing a typeface that immediately reminded Tim of the warning sent to Douglas Grant, read as follows:

ZIPPA,

IF YOU CONTINUE TO SNOOP, IT WON'T BE A PLASTIC HEAD IN THIS OVEN. IT'LL BE <u>YOUR</u> HEAD.

PACK UP AND GO. LEAVE NOW, OR DIE.

TELL YOUR FRIENDS, ONE BLACK AND ONE WHITE, THAT TO STAY HERE MORE THAN TWO DAYS MEANS I WILL HAVE TO KILL THEM.

Chapter Nineteen

In every community, those who feel the burdens of taxation are naturally prone to relieve themselves from their fiscal discomfort. One class struggles to throw the burden off its shoulders. If they succeed, of course it must fall upon others. They also, in their turn, labor to get rid of it, and finally the load falls upon those who will not, or cannot, make a successful effort for relief.
                              J.C. Carter
                              T.S. Adams

On Friday morning, Tim and Martin spent an hour with Sheriff Kruger. "June's over in seven days," the sheriff noted. "You making any progress on finding the killer?"
"Not enough."
"Neither is Nagle." The sheriff picked up the note and reread it for the tenth time. "You know something, Martin? This matter doesn't concern you or any of your relatives. You could pull out of this and leave town. Nobody would think any less of you."
"You really think you can make me leave town?" Martin asked with thinly veiled defiance.
"No, I sure don't. The counterweight is, I'm not at all sure I can keep you alive if you stay."
"Life has its little risks," Martin replied calmly.
"Fine. Stay." The sheriff tapped his fingers on his desk. "The words 'one black' have obvious reference to Shawn Sparlin. This is the first time he's been threatened. I see no intelligent reason why it can't be the last, since I have it on good authority that he's not nearly as stubborn as you two. He even enjoys leaving Greenharbor. New Orleans, New York...he's a traveler. So..." the sheriff waited until Tim's eyes met his... "if you want to do something decent, convince him to leave town. For at least three weeks."
"I'll try. I see your point and I agree with it. But I'm not sure Shawn will buy it."
The sheriff rubbed his forehead. He sounded tired and he looked tired.
"I suggest you try right now. Mr. Sumoto and I are going to have a little chat about restaurant security. While we tend to that lofty matter, you could be saving a soul brother's life---if in fact the idiot who writes these notes actually plans to kill again."

                         * * *

Before going to see Shawn, Tim checked with his aunt to see if he had any messages. He learned that he had received a phone call from Novia Dixon, urging Tim to meet her at the Greenharbor Little Theater as soon as he could get there.

When he arrived at the theater, Tim found Novia sitting at her cluttered desk. She motioned Tim into a chair, and thanked him for coming.

"I know that you're keenly concerned with the murder of Sid Burk. Tim, I believe quite earnestly that I have some new information for you."

"You have my undivided attention, Novia."

"First of all, I want to repeat something that everyone keeps forgetting. Sid Burk died at four p.m. on May the twenty-fifth. Four p.m. I wasn't there. I was here in this very office at four p.m. and I have a witness to prove it. I got there about five forty-five and came right back. My car practically never left my sight, and it could not possibly have made the tracks by you uncle's barn."

"I'm not questioning your account of events, Novia."

She looked at him with the frailest of smiles. "Do you think Martin feels that way? Or deep down, does he really suspect I was involved?"

"Maybe I shouldn't say so, but between you and me, he seems to be confident of your innocence."

Her smile brightened a little, then faded. "Tim, my location or whereabouts was old news for you, but I appreciate your hearing me out. Now quite seriously I do have some recent information."

"Involving one of the remaining five?"

"Yes. Have you considered what a predicament Elston Grant finds himself in? Why, even the newspaper picked up on the two pieces of land going to him. Can't you see the box he's in? He doesn't dare sell any of that land for a profit. Tongues would wag, and it would hurt his image."

"Meaning..."

"I'm suggesting that Elston Grant will have to sell that land for less than it's worth. That gives him a defense, because surely he wouldn't murder someone just to sell their property for peanuts. What else can he do?"

"And..."

"And he'll sell that land, in due course of time, through a real estate agent. Verna Barger. But will anybody notice what she makes on the deal? What she and a scheming behind-the-scenes partner might divide as booty?"

Tim frowned slightly. "One might get the impression that Burk's land was covered with gold mines and oil wells. Why kill somebody just to make a few thousand?"

"People have killed for less. Besides, Ling tells me that he was first given a lower figure for Orick Farm, then---the day Burk was killed---a higher figure. I think Burk tried to raise the price when he learned a wealthy businessman wanted it. That soured the deal, because Ling wasn't about to be held up."

"Uh...it turned his 'sweet pickles to dill,' as I remember the phrase."

"Yes. Burk's squeeze play for a fast profit was costing Verna money, damaging her rapport with an important client, and infuriating her. I think she shot Burk with the hope that his mother would sell both pieces of land for next to nothing. When she balked..."

"So if Molly Burk had signed the codicil with Douglas and Jane not much before Verna's visit...the incriminating inheritance would've fallen into place."

"Certainly."

"But...could Verna Barger have moved Sid Burk's body all by herself?"

"She's no weakling. Besides, there are jacks and similar devices that allow somebody to lift more weight than she could lift by herself."

"I suppose so. But as your theory stands, Novia, it's a loosely tied string of ifs and maybes. Any other evidence?"

"Yes. This very morning I dropped some papers off at Verna's office, for a friend. I had to wait until Verna got off the phone." Novia leaned forward. "I distinctly heard her say, 'That's right, Elston. It's not as much money as you might have wanted. But it'll make you look better.'"

Chapter Twenty

The principal role of the General Fixed Assets Account Group (GFAAG) is to provide proper accounting control over general fixed assets. In addition to providing for efficient and effective usage, control over general fixed assets is necessary to safeguard such assets. Significantly, the GFAAG also provides information required to implement capital improvement programs and capital budgeting activities.
  Michael S. Luehlfing

On Saturday morning Tim, Martin and Shawn met at the Whinney farmhouse to review the list of suspects.

"First of all," Tim said, "do you see any way that the eight-suspects-only theory might be incorrect?"

There was silence for almost a minute. Then Martin spoke. "It almost has to be right. Agreed that the killer could've walked overland or dove through the cave. Then, it could be that he or she stole a car to move the body. But the car went back to its original spot. None of the vehicles had blood, mud or water in the trunk or passenger area---the sheriff is resolutely certain about that. So, we would be forced to believe that the killer hangs around a stolen car for goodness-knows-how-long, carefully cleaning it up. What for? It's senseless."

"So you're saying," Shawn commented, "that one of eight dudes did it, and had to clean his own buggy, just in case the stags came snooping."

"Yes."

"My thinking matches yours," Tim added. "I can see somebody sneaking past a deputy one way---going in, perhaps---but both ways? And Rankin said the deputies were straighter than Baptist pokers."

"Hold on. Why are we taking Rankin's word for it? If he's the killer, he could've bribed a deputy."

"Yeah...the fox speaking up for the ferret."

"Well, guys, double-check him if you want to. Kruger knows his men, and he's no fool. He puts his money on them. Besides, if a deputy stepped into the brush briefly, he would've *heard* a vehicle...the muddy tracks would've stayed there."

"One other thought," Martin interjected. "We've all seen pickups with the body jacked up extra high above the wheels. Sometimes they have oversized tires. Why couldn't a vehicle like that come in the *north* way, staying on the pavement and plowing through the deep water?"

"I looked into that. You may have noticed that there are two old posts on either side of the roadway, up where the high water point was. When the deputies closed the north loop, they ran a chain from one post to the other, and locked it in place. If the lock had been broken or the chain cut, that would've been obvious. A tall truck might've braved three feet of water and gone around the posts, but once again there would've been huge ruts."

"Agreed," Martin said.

Tim continued, "Just how much do we know about these six people? What about Douglas? He's a nice guy, and he almost got killed, but do we know why the killer despises him?"

"Or if," Shawn said.

"How's that?"

"People can send themselves notes. People can hire a marksman to nick a car roof."

"Oh, theoretically, yes. But if you ask me, he'd be a fool to hire some militaristic crazy to come within inches of blowing off his head. What's to keep the guy from giving matters a morbid twist and forgetting to miss?"

"I'm with Tim. I can't see Doug teaming up with someone else. Not unless it would be one of those classy females he dates."

"Speaking of class-act women, Martin, tell me about Novia. She says she has a witness who can place her at the theater at exactly four p.m. Is it true?"

"Yes and no. Her witness is Jane Potter, who remains on vacation in Canada."

"Hold it! Hold it!" Shawn waved his hand. "When we talked this out on Tuesday night, Martin, you said Novia never mentioned Jane as her alibi *until* the robin flew off to Canada."

"Well let's nail down the loose flooring. Without Jane, does Novia have any witness that she stayed in Greenharbor until five-thirty or so?"

"No."

"But do either of you think Novia is guilty?"

"Count me out for that one," Shawn replied.

"I don't believe for a minute that she did it. For one thing, where's the motive? If she were greedy for the money, why would she be hanging around Greenharbor?"

"We don't yet have a clear motive." Tim jotted down some notes. "Next is Verna Barger. Anybody suspect her?"

"She's the one you'd least suspect," replied Shawn. "Therefore, I vote we watch her."

"She's not much of a prospect."

"But Martin, Novia has a notion that..."

"Forget it. When two very different women don't like each other, some halfbaked gossip pies are likely to get thrown. Let's stay clear of the inedible debris."

"Two people are left. Do either of you think Ling Sumoto has or could have a motive?"

"No," said Shawn. "There's no way Ling would lose his temper over anything Sid Burk would do."

"Agreed."

"Well, guys, up to this point, everybody's innocent," Tim said. "But there's one name left---Elston Grant."

"He was good to my parents," Shawn said softly. "Good to a lot of blacks in this town. He defended a few of them for free. I vote not guilty, on general character."

"Martin?"

"He's in an awkward situation, inheriting all that land. So awkward, in fact, that I think somebody else supplied the frame for that picture."

Before they adjourned, Tim reviewed all of the written evidence, including notes and photocopies. Then their consultation ended, with Shawn leaving to visit his friend Harry.

Tim was in a mood to interview any available witnesses. At the county law enforcement building, he learned that Sheriff Kruger was taking this Saturday off. Tim was almost out of the building when he crossed paths with Deputy Wade Nagle.

"Well, well! If it isn't Professor Whinney." As usual, Nagle's voice was tinged with sarcasm. "How's your top-secret investigation going?"

"Slowly, to tell you the truth. You know that Douglas Grant and I were shot at?"

"I heard."

"Surely that's had some influence on your thinking about my uncle and aunt's innocence?"

"Maybe yes and maybe no. If the rifleman out by your farm just has to be the killer, then sure, your uncle may be off the hook. But the Grants are rich and rich folk have enemies. Lawyers and their helpers have enemies. Burk's killer used a .38 pistol, as best we can tell. That ain't no rifle. Unless of course you want to modify your story and say that some man with a .38 shot at you two. I suppose you could tell the sounds apart, couldn't you?"

"Of course I could. I'm not a dope. I grew up in the country with hunting weapons all around me. Whoever fired at us used a rifle, or at least something

higher-pitched than a .38."
 "All right...let's not argue about it. I will concede that your uncle appears slightly less guilty now." Nagle dropped his voice to a whisper. "Between you and me and the wise old owl, I'm keeping close tabs on Elston Grant."
 "I'll...certainly keep that quiet." Tim stepped on out to the street, not sure of how to deal with Nagle's confidence.

* * *

 Martin completed his work at six p.m. that Saturday, primarily because the municipal building was closing early for some long-scheduled maintenance. After stopping by the Whinney farm to pick up Tim, Martin drove to Sparlin Farm. Shawn was home, and soon the three of them headed for Shawn's pond with their new scuba gear. Both Tim and Martin had bought full neoprene wetsuits.
 "Look, Shawn," asked Tim, "can we go into the cave today?"
 "Don't thing so. Neither of you is up to cave diving yet, but we can to the entrance," Shawn said. "To go cave diving, we need dive lights. Either of you could panic inside the cave. Where the cave exits on the river, the currents are rough. We'll get to Hawaii to dive. Trust me."
 "Hawaii would be nice," Martin replied, or "Grand Cayman."
 "Besides," Shawn said, "I don't want either of you to be eaten by alligators."
 "Alligators?" Tim almost shouted.
 Shawn smiled and said, "Just joking. Remind me to tell you about swimming with sharks."
 "Hey," Martin said, "there are a lot of sharks in the accounting profession. Very competitive. What's the sign for a shark anyway?" Martin was referring to the series of hand signals that divers use to communicate underwater.
 Shawn asked if they knew the reason a diver carries a knife. Both Martin and Tim shook their heads.
 "In case you see a shark, you scan use the knife to stab you buddies." Shawn gave his silly smile.
 Both Tim and Martin dove with their new wetsuits. Now they would stay warm, even at the bottom of the pond. They explored the entrance of the cave, using Shawn's dive light. The cave did not appear natural and Shawn had said that the previous pond designer had gone to great trouble to add a passage to the Ohio River.

After about thirty minutes on the bottom they ascended slowly. The trio broke the surface of the pond, after their three minute safety stop at fifteen feet below the surface. Shawn required the safety stop to ensure that there was no chance of the bends. While diving with compressed air, the body accumulates nitrogen in the body. Ascending too rapidly causes nitrogen bubbles, much as opening a soda pop after shaking it. The longer and deeper the dive, the longer the safety stop needed.

Shawn told them about diving with dozens of sting-rays at Sting-ray City on Grand Cayman. The rays would actually bump into the divers, demanding to be fed squid.

"But let me tell you my most exciting dive at Walker's Cay, on a small island off the Florida coast," Shawn said. "As soon as the boat got to the spot, sharks knew it was feeding time. You could see them from the boat. We jumped into the water and descended rapidly thirty feet to the sandy bottom.

"Once we were on the bottom, the boat roared its motor to call more sharks. Then, the boat lowered a large frozen mass of fish—called a chumcicle. The sharks went wild feeding on the frozen fish. There must have been a hundred sharks. They would swim within a couple of feet of us. I touched two sharks," Shawn related.

"But I've never seen a humpback whale. Did you know that humpbacks are federally protected?" Shawn asked Tim. "We really must plan our trip to Hawaii to the the humpbacks before I die."

The diving and stories were refreshing, and all of the recent stress seemed to evaporate.

Tim sat half-immersed in the blue water after removing his equipment and wetsuit, reclining lazily on an inflated inner tube. Casually he watched Shawn stand near the deepest drop-off and execute a clean, graceful dive.

"Eden could've been like this," Martin said two minutes later. "Magic. Serene."

"That could be future, as well as past." Shawn stared at some distant view. "Maybe the three of us will be together in a place like Eden."

Tim saw a gleam of light at the other end of the pond, which he took to be a reflection from the sun.

"We've got work to do this coming week. Martin, it may get busy enough that we'll have to break you loose from the audit caper."

"Just say the word. Clearing your uncle and aunt is my top priority."

"I know. Shawn, we'll keep you busy, too."

"I'm gonna help, one way or another."

"We could stay here for hours," Martin remarked as he turned sideways to face his comrades.

"Not me," Shawn replied. "You're both great company, but I've got an invitation to go play my guitar where they truly appreciate music."

That moment froze in time. At any age---thirty, forty, fifty---Tim knew he could instantly recall the trees, the pond, the handsome countenance with a drop of water running off Shawn's chin and catching the sunlight as it curved and reached a glistening stop in the middle of his chest. Freeze frame. End of video.

The shot rang out from the opposite bank. It was too loud, too close, too frightening for immediate reaction. Martin was the first to act. He flung himself backwards, reaching out to pull Tim away from the line of fire. "My god! Get down!"

But even as he was pulled backwards, Tim understood what the bullet had done. Pulling free from his friend's grasp, he lunged forward. He grabbed Shawn in his arms, but there was no response.

As Martin once again jerked Tim into a lower and safer position, they could both see Shawn's ugly head wound, the pool of red water, the lifeless body. Martin stared at the trees on the opposite bank, and saw a human figure running. Running. Giving up his murderous advantage. His bravery spent, his cowardice restored, running. Martin jumped up and leaped for the shore. There was a chance of overtaking him. Tim cradled Shawn's limp body for a few moments, then decided to float him to the shore.

The wound was too accurate, too obviously centered through the brain to permit the least hope of survival.

"Oh god! God in heaven, why?" Tim reached the bank, held the body, and felt a choking scream escape from his throat. "Shawn!"

With all his heart Tim wanted to cry, but no tears came. His lip quivered, his hands turned slippery with blood, but tears were beyond his grasp. And where *could* he turn, at a moment like this? The killer running, Martin chasing, and Tim sitting.

He stood up, looking toward the tallest tree as blood dripped off his arms. "Is he going home to see his parents? Are they the ones he meant, who would truly appreciate his music?"

Then Tim knelt by the silent body, and slowly touched his fingers to Shawn's neck. There was no heartbeat, and the flow of blood slowed. As if in reprimand, Tim shook his finger at his friend's body.

"In a few short years, we will continue this

conversation."

Tim splashed into the water to wash off the blood, then emerged near his clothing. He noticed that Martin's pants were gone. Dressing as fast as he could, Tim turned one last time in the direction of the body.

"Our friendship goes on, uninterrupted. Not even death can stop that."

Fully dressed, Tim grabbed the rest of Martin's clothing and ran after him.

Chapter Twenty-one

A budget is a financial plan describing proposed expenditures and the means of financing them. Budgets typically play a far greater role in planning and controlling governmental operations than they do in the private sector.
                                Karen S. McKenzie

Tim caught up to Martin at Shawn's house, where the Zippa convertible was parked under the oak tree. Martin was struggling to pull a wooden board away from the front tires.

"He got away?" Tim asked as he stopped to catch his breath, and dropped Martin's clothes on the hood of the car.

"I thought I had him. I took one wrong turn on that trail, which cost me maybe...four seconds. When I got here I could still see the dust in the air...but the creep had protected himself with these nail-spiked boards, wedged against my tires."

"Punctured?"

"No. Just too much delay to catch him." Martin freed the large, nail-spangled chunk of wood, and tossed it aside. "We can roll now. Any hope for him?"

They knew each other well. The tone of the question implied that the answer was known. Tim wouldn't have paused for two questions if he were racing against time to save a life. The race was over.

"You might as well get dressed, Martin. Then we can see who's home at Grant's house, and maybe use their phone."

* * *

At the Grant household they found Elston Grant, dressed in a sport shirt and casual slacks, in the middle of a light meal.

"Hello, Dr. Whinney. And Mr. Zippa. What brings you by?"

"A tragedy, I'm afraid." Tim paused a moment. "Is...Doug here?"

"No. No, he's visiting some friends in Greenharbor. Spends a good deal of his time there, actually."

"Then you're alone," Martin concluded. "There's no proof as to where you were, ten minutes ago."

Tim's right hand touched Martin's chest ever so gently, in a signal not to pursue an interrogation. "Mr. Grant, we need to use the phone. There's been a

shooting. Our mutual neighbor, Shawn Sparlin, is dead."
The color seemed to drain from Elston Grant's face. "Oh no. No. Not again." He pointed to a nearby telephone. "Please, make the call."

* * *

It is no doubt unusual for someone's next of kin to be a first cousin, but that was the situation which placed Lyda Sparlin in charge of Shawn's funeral and his estate. Knowing this, Tim braced himself for what he thought would be the second worst experience of the day. It was nine p.m.
"We've got to do it, Martin. I've got to talk to Lyda."
"It'll be hard for both of you. I hate to see you put yourself through this."
"Some things have to be done."
After some brief preparation, Martin and Tim went by themselves to see Lyda.
Inside, Tim walked past several visitors to find Lyda, kiss her cheek, and give her a brief hug. She was calm and composed.
"I'm glad you came, Tim. I'd like your advice on planning the funeral."
She sat down in a comfortable chair, and an elderly friend held her hand. "You'll all have to understand that this was not a great shock to me. I've known it was coming for years. And Shawn knew. He knew he would have a short life. It seemed to affect everything he did."
Martin stood behind the folding chair. "Lyda, is there anything we can do to help *you*?"
"No, I'm fine. But before you have to leave, let me tell you something. The last time Shawn spoke with me, yesterday afternoon, he mentioned you. Tim in particular. I'll try to quote him. He said you had 'no veneer. He's good to the core. His dreams are a gift, and he'll be a great person some day.' I thought it was a grand thing for Shawn to say."
"Undeserved, I'm sure. He was a prince, Lyda. I'll miss him, but more importantly I'll try to live up to his opinion of me."

* * *

Monday was not as hard to face as Tim had thought it would be. As he woke up, he reasoned within himself that he should have been feeling anger and overwhelming loss. But instead, the serenity of that pond had somehow been transferred to him. His sense of peace was coupled with a dedication to find a triple killer and prevent any more deaths. "If that's possible," Tim whispered to himself as he shaved. "I can't control everything. Shawn told me that more than once."

Tim spent an hour that morning talking to the sheriff, and noting that Kruger was *not* serene.

"These murders are beginning to upset me." Sheriff Kruger was starting to ramble. "If I ever get my hands on this...this..." After a moment of silence, the Sheriff said, "I've sent word to the FBI. We may have a serial killer on our hands."

"Sheriff, please. I understand your feelings. I have no desire to pin a merit badge on this person either. But we've got to face reality and admit that we're dealing with a simple money motive and the person could kill again. And possibly soon. We need to control our energy and direct it toward correct interpretation of the evidence, and an arrest."

"Well of course." The sheriff frowned, and glanced from the window he was staring out of to Tim, then back to the window. "Why are you talking like that? You were personally involved with the latest victim, and I expected you to turn into a basket case."

"Sorry to disappoint you, but I'm made out of sterner stuff than that. Now, did you recover the bullet?"

"Yes we did. Ballistics says we might do well to look for a Remington 552. You'll recall that our friend Dawson didn't actually *sell* a gun to anybody; he just came up with a missing form. Well, to add fuel to the fire, we now have a report of a stolen 552, taken in a Marietta burglary the night of June thirteenth."

Tim blinked. "If a Remington 552 killed Shawn, and that weapon turns up in my uncle's possession..."

"Then he'll be in one heck of a mess."

"Oh brother. What a headache."

"Item two. Deputy Nagle wants a word with you."

Kruger pushed his intercom buzzer. "Send Nagle in."

When Deputy Nagle entered the office, Sheriff Kruger stood up. "Gentlemen, I have pressing business. Have a nice chat."

Nagle sat down in a chair about five feet from Tim. "Uh...I wanted to let you know...that I'm very sorry about Shawn's death. He...uh..used to play music at a couple of places where I'd stop for a drink, so we knew each other. He was a nice guy. Talented, too. I heard that you and he and Zippa were getting to be good friends. So...uh...I know it hurts, watching someone die in front of you. I really am sorry."

"Thank you, Deputy."

"If you ever want to talk about losing someone close, I've got credentials. As you may know...my wife died in a car accident two years ago."

"I didn't know."

"That was rough. Maybe if I'm sometimes a little caustic, well... truth is, I'm still a touch bitter about losing her."

Tim sat back in his chair. "Yeah...maybe we could talk about that. About getting hurt."

* * *

Shortly after twelve, Tim parked his car on the north side of the Whinney house, across the driveway from their garage. He met Martin inside, and ten minutes later they left in the convertible, to keep a luncheon appointment with Novia Dixon.

It was nearing two o'clock as the young men returned to the farm. Clouds were gathering, and the possibility of rain was increasing.

"Go on in, Martin. I'm going to put the windows up in my uncle's car."

Tim opened the sedan's driver side door and was cranking away when he saw the rifle. It was lying there, in the front seat---a Remington 552.

"Oh, no. No, this isn't happening." For a few moments he leaned against the open car door, trying to decide how to respond. He was within a second of picking up the weapon when a sheriff's patrol car pulled into the driveway.

Tim knew his uncle didn't need to be found in possession of a murder weapon. The young man jumped into the front seat and rolled the window back down, as the two deputies began walking toward him. Because his body didn't cover the length of the weapon, which was jammed uncomfortably against his upper hips, Tim raised his right leg and stretched it across the seat. He knew he would look ridiculous in such a pose, but he hoped that with a smile and a casual air it would somehow come off.

"You're Tim Whinney, aren't you?"

"Yes...yes that's right."

"We've had a tip that some startling evidence could be found in your yard...or your garage."

"Really?" Tim boosted his casual facade up to the maximum. "Well, it's probably just some nosy neighbor thinking out loud. You know how tempting it is for folks to horn in on a murder investigation."

"Maybe so. However, we would appreciate your

permission to look around."

"Oh certainly. Go right ahead. We have nothing to hide. No cover-ups here."

Tim looked to his left and saw Martin standing by the house. Frantically, Tim waved his comrade closer.

"Something wrong with your leg, Dr. Whinney?"

"No. No. Just a little muscle cramp. Goes right away if I hold my leg out straight."

Martin arrived at the car window. "Tim, your aunt wants to see you."

"Oh there's no time for that, Martin. We've got to...uh...deliver the painting that Mr. Sumoto bought."

"What painting?"

"You remember...the expensive one he's been expecting. Just came in, and he can't wait to get it. So if you'll *please get in*, we'll deliver it right away." Tim turned his attention back to the deputies. "You guys look anywhere you wish. The lawn, the garage, the two barns...help yourselves. Have a good search."

"Thank you, Dr. Whinney."

Taking no chances, Tim pulled his leg back to the gas pedal only when Martin was landing on the passenger's side.

Grateful that the keys were in the car, Tim started the engine as the deputies stepped back. "Later, fellows. Give my best to the sheriff."

It was after three minutes of driving that Tim let out a deep breath and brought the car to a stop. Having satisfied themselves that no one was watching, they examined the rifle as they stood by the car trunk.

"Probably the murder weapon, and probably wiped clean of prints. But if we turn it in, and there's one print that we didn't catch, somebody would be headed for a jury trial."

"A clever person can lift someone's prints, copy them on plastic and put them on another surface. If this madman has gone to those lengths...no, I can't do that to my uncle."

"Your uncle! Maybe *your* prints are on that gun. Or maybe mine. Wouldn't that be great? They arrest me for the murder, discount your testimony and waste no time in convicting me. The sheriff *is* eager to solve this case, isn't he?"

"Not that way. I think he'd see through it. But you raise a chilling possibility. The killer's free to make anyone look guilty."

"Deliberation is closed." Martin shut the trunk lid. "Let's stash it for now."

"Where would it be safe?"

"How about...Vince Corbett's basement?"

The rifle was entrusted to their friend and faculty colleague, Vince Corbett. The long-term plan was to have the lab at Ohio University examine the weapon.

The next day brought Shawn's funeral. It was a brief and low-key service. Tim looked around the room and noticed all of the eight original suspects in the room, except for Verna Barger. That meant, to his disgust, that the odds were high that Shawn's murderer was attending the service.

As soon as the funeral ended, and Tim and Martin had completed their duties as pallbearers, they spoke briefly to Lyda and several of Shawn's friends, and then made their exit.

In spite of his feelings of dejection, Tim managed a smile. "He knew how to live, didn't he? Whatever comes after this world...I bet he's handling it just fine."

* * *

That evening at the Whinney farm, Tim answered a phone call from Sheriff Kruger.

"Good evening, Sheriff. Did your men find anything of merit in yesterday's search?"

"Nothing, Tim. I hope that wasn't an inconvenience. Guess we've reached the grasping-at-straws stage."

"Or shooting in the dark, to turn a phrase."

"That wasn't why I called. Tim, did you know that Sparlin Farm was part of a trust, initiated by Shawn's parents?"

"No. I simply assumed that Shawn owned the place."

"No he didn't. He had a lifetime right to use the property, but not to sell it. With his death, ownership is transferred to the Martin Luther King Foundation of Greenharbor."

"You mean...some charitable entity now owns Sparlin Farm?"

"Yes. Everyone has been content to leave it at that, until Deputy Nagle and I put our heads together and decided to flesh out every last detail."

"I think you're trying to tell me something."

"You're right. This MLK Foundation, as they call it for short, is an older, less active organization managed by five or six elderly black citizens. To be quite blunt, they're up in years, they seldom meet, and the board of directors or trustees seldom make decisions."

"Who does?"

"That's precisely the question that needed to be asked. The foundation's executive director runs the show, and for all intent and purposes, he'll decide

exactly what to do with Sparlin Farm."
 "Who is he?"
 "Surely you've guessed. Attorney Elston Grant is the executive director, and therefore now has control of four adjacent pieces of land on the Old Nelson Road."

Chapter Twenty-two

While PPBS [Planning, Programming, Budgeting Systems] has not produced the formal analyses of all means and ends, or the realistic planning and program structures envisioned by the reformers, the case of AID demonstrates that significant agencies tried to improve their performance (either before Congress or in the field) via development of some to its features.
                              George M. Guess

On Wednesday morning, Tim and Martin responded to an invitation from Lyda and met with her and her attorney at Lyda's modest cottage in Greenharbor. Bruce Evanson, her attorney, was an industrious black in his thirties. Early in the meeting, the lawyer accepted a glass of lemonade from Lyda as he glanced around the small house.
"It's a nice place, Lyda. You've done the best you can with what you've got. But let me tell you something. Sparlin Farm should be yours. I've done a little research, and I've learned that in the 1920s only four families owned land up there. The Nelsons, the Shumways, the Sparlins, and the Oricks. The Sparlins were probably the first blacks to own any land around here. It gave them some status when that was a rare commodity for blacks. You're a Sparlin. That farm, or what's left of it, should be yours."
"Maybe." Lyda handed glasses to Tim and Martin. "My uncle and aunt gave the property to a foundation. It's all written and legal. Who's to stop it, and by what right?"
Tim asked, "Did Shawn's parents ever tell you exactly what they planned to do with their property?"
She gave it a moment's thought. "No, I don't suppose so."
"I'll tell you my theory," Tim continued. "I think his parents reasoned that sooner or later Shawn would take his guitar and move to a big city. If by chance he stayed here, and died of old age, you'd be even older, so why list *you* as an alternate heir? Maybe they were concentrating on the land when they should've thought more about unexpected death and family needs."
"*Assuming*, Tim, that this title transfer is genuine."
"Thank you, Martin."
Bruce tapped his lemonade glass against Martin's in a makeshift toast. "I was hoping somebody else might be as suspicious as I am."
"Well, the sheriff said it looked legal. Mr.

Grant's secretary, Thelma, sent me a copy of the letter where he accepted the property." Lyda turned to Tim. "Have you seen it?"

"No. Have you got it here?"

"I surely do."

"Then why don't we all read it together? It might tell us some things that we don't know now."

Tim, Martin and Bruce bunched together like a huddled football team as Lyda spread the letter out on her kitchen table.

The missive was written on stationery from the Martin Luther King Foundation of Greenharbor. The date indicated that the letter had been composed six years earlier.

> Dear Mr. and Mrs. Sparlin,
>
> I am writing by way of expressing appreciation for the gift of your property. By establishing a remainder trust, you are emphasizing your commitment to the Martin Luther King Foundation of Greenharbor. You are setting an example and lighting a torch that others will surely see. By contributing your cherished farm---exempting of course those years that Shawn will reside there---you are expressing a commitment to educational opportunity. Saluting your wisdom is the least I can do.
>
> Making this gift shows foresight on your part. By opening doors, creating patterns for others and enlightening the future's pathway, you serve Dr. King's memory and his ideals. All of us at MLK-F are gratified by your providing this compassionate legacy.
>
> Cordially,
> Elston Grant

"So here we have a genuine Elston Grant letter," Tim remarked when no one spoke.

Lyda asked, "What is a *trust*?"

Tim said, "A trust is a fiduciary relationship with respect to property, subjecting the person holding title to the property to equitable duties in dealing with the property for the benefit of another person. There are often three parties to a trust. The grantor was your uncle and aunt, the trustee is Elston Grant, the present beneficiary was Shawn, and the future beneficiary is the MLK Foundation."

Martin suggested that the paperwork was sound tax-wise. "Except for a remainder interest in a residence or farm, no charitable deduction is allowed for a gift in the future. Thus, your aunt and uncle did get a charitable deduction on their individual tax return or their estate tax return---assuming they itemized their deductions."

Tim corrected Martin, "You are assuming that the MLK Foundation is a qualified charitable organization under the tax laws. I hope so. In general, Lyda, a trust is not a taxable entity *if* the trust income is distributed to the beneficiaries. That's called a simple trust. As a conduit, the distributed income is taxed to the beneficiaries."

"I imagine the foundation has Section 501(c)(3) status, which would give it tax exempt status by the IRS and make all contributions it receives tax deductible to the donor," said Martin. "If so, the files should contain Form 1023, an application for recognition of exemption and annual tax returns on Form 990. We can check on that letter. What about the Elston Grant connection?"

Bruce inspected the wording again, and frowned. "Boy am I skeptical. 'Lighting a torch,' he says...I'm going to light a torch under Grant...and that's a promise."

"I'm sure Mr. Grant will rapidly reach the conclusion that he's being watched," Martin speculated.

* * *

By Friday Tim knew he had to have a respite from shadowing Elston Grant, retracing the man's activities and searching for undisclosed economic motivation. For an evening's diversion, he escorted Lisa to the premier of *The Olympian Circle*, presented by the Greenharbor Little Theater. Martin took his own car and met them in the theater's lobby.

Before the lights went down, the trio had a chance to chat about the play.

"You seem to know a lot about it," Lisa told Tim. "Have you been to some of the rehearsals?"

"Not one. But I can't wait to ogle the goddesses."

The play highlighted the Greek deities Zeus, Apollo and Hera. Assisted by their lesser divine cohorts, the three celestial leaders engaged in combat with the frost giants under Ymir's command.

Lisa was impressed with the cast. "Mmm...the actor playing Zeus has a body that would drive a Greek god to jealousy. Perfect casting."

"Hera has a few well-placed curves, herself."

On stage, while Apollo held off the enemies with his

mighty arrows, Zeus contemplated why the opposition had gained so much power. At last he figured it out---the great circle that hung above the stage and represented Olympian power was in reality a false and incomplete circle. It was an unfinished loop; its circumference did not fully close. Zeus explained to Hera that they had seen what they expected to see, and closed the circle with their eyes when it was in cold fact not closed, not a circle, and not an adequate defense against frost giants or agents of deception. In the nick of time Zeus and Apollo found the true Olympian circle, and justice prevailed as the final curtain came down.

The Greenharbor audience rewarded the cast with a standing ovation. As the dozens of patrons began their slow but steady exodus, Tim and Lisa paused for a moment near a drinking fountain.

She asked, "Shouldn't we see if Martin would like to have a hamburger with us?"

"Uh, I understand that Martin has some plans of his own. That's why he's lingering backstage."

* * *

Bruce Evanston passed up the chance to attend the theater in order to complete his work on two upcoming court cases. Alone in his Greenharbor office, he finished a final page of notes, then closed the loose-leaf notebook.

Turning on a small lamp at his library desk, he examined the map which Tim Whinney had given him earlier in the day. It underscored the fact that one domino after another had fallen, and now Elston Grant owned or controlled four adjacent pieces of property. Too much blood had flowed for that fact to be insignificant.

"This map tells a good story, but it's not quite expressive enough to reveal the ultimate truth." He put the map inside his briefcase and began turning off all the lights.

Outside the building, he walked some thirty feet to his car, vaguely noticing that the streetlight had burned out and the area was darker than usual. He fumbled with his door key, slowed in part by darkness and in part by an old and reluctant lock mechanism.

When he glanced upward, it was to make sure that the key he was struggling with was the right one. His eyes caught the silent advance of a darkened car, bearing down on him with increasing speed. With less than two seconds to spare, Bruce leaped atop the hood of his own vehicle as the unlit car torpedoed past, scraping

Bruce's front bumper and launching his briefcase high into the air.

Three seconds later, all was quiet. Bruce contemplated sliding off the hood as a security guard ambled onto the street.

"Something wrong out here?"

Bruce hopped to a standing position. "Yes, something's wrong. I've just found out that standing in Elston Grant's way is an invitation to get killed."

Chapter Twenty-three

Cost accounting is a speciality within general business accounting; government contract accounting is a speciality within cost accounting.
                                        James P. Bedingfield
                                        Louis I. Rosen

Sally Reed spotted Martin using his laptop computer at his work desk. "What are you up to, Martin?"

"Hi, Sally. I'm checking the internet for current accounting and auditing events that could affect the audit. I'm almost finished with the audit, but there may be new items I should know about. I make it a practice to surf the net before I complete all my audits. The most up-to-date accounting information now is available on the net.

"I started by checking the AICPA homepage. The AICPA has over a thousand pages on the net. The audit guidelines that I follow come from the AICPA industry audit guide on state and local governmental units and the Statements on Auditing Standards. They don't indicate any new procedures that would influence this audit. The Government Accounting Standards Board still has a Preliminary Views document outstanding on the government reporting model. That's really important, but it won't affect this audit. It looks like more federal guidelines will be coming in the future.

"I couldn't find a web page for Greenharbor. Did I miss it?"

"No," said Sally. "We've talked about it, but decided against it because of the cost. Do you think it's important?"

"Yes. Most bigger cities and tourist area have web pages now, some quite extensive. Greenharbor probably needs one sooner or later. As an auditor, there is the possibility of extracting important information. But mainly, I'm just curious. What information is presented and why? Eventually there can be considerable information presented and real dialog between the city's managers and voters."

                    *   *   *

On Monday, the third of July, Chief Deputy Wade Nagle drove to Elston Grant's house, hoping to discuss several matters with the attorney. No one answered the front door, but it was unlocked. Nagle entered the house, and soon learned why Elston Grant did not answer the door. The lawyer's blood-splattered body was slumped over his desk in the first-floor study.

The logical inference was that Elston Grant had committed suicide. A .38 revolver was in his right hand, with one cartridge fired. A blood-encrusted note was in his typewriter, explaining in some detail the rationale for three murders.

Two hours later, with the original letter safely locked in the evidence room, Sheriff Kruger reread his photocopy of the message. He looked up from his desk to the silent face of Deputy Nagle. "This suicide should do it, Wade. The end of the nightmare."

"Hallelujah. That's a load off everyone's shoulders."

"To say the least." The sheriff stretched his arms. "I'm ready to take a week off and go fishing. The wife and I haven't gone anywhere since the start of the flood."

"Some flood," Nagle reflected somberly. "Funny how high water tends to drive the vermin into your front yard."

Sheriff Kruger tossed the photocopy onto his desk. "It's time to decommission Tim Whinney. He can go back to academic life and forget about crime detection."

Forty minutes later, Tim and Martin walked into the sheriff's office. Martin looked relieved. Tim's expression was more one of disbelief tinged with exasperation.

"Is it true? Grant left a note confessing *everything*?"

"Right. He confessed more than we could prove the killer had actually done." The sheriff pointed to his desk. "I suppose you'd like to read that."

"Seeing as how I've got nothing better to do." Once more, Tim held an important paper and Martin hovered near his partner's shoulder.

> I am trapped in a canyon from which there is no escape. Before I end this agony, I want to apologize to all of you. It was not my original plan to hurt you, and yet my clumsiness has caused me to devastate your lives.
>
> What led me to kill Sid Burk? And then to poison Molly Burk, and finally to expand my murderous grasp to include Shawn Sparlin? I won't force you to guess: it was my lifelong obsession to bring a Grant estate back into existence.
>
> Few of you can recall that my grandfather

owned hundreds of acres. All of my life I reached for that goal, thirsted for it, yet never had enough money to realize it. Temptation yielded to avarice, and both surrendered to bloodrampancy.

What led me to frame Everett Whinney? Simply his availability...he was a most available decoy. In my cleverness I found it wise to transplant the toolbox and to plant the rifle in Whinney's car.

Once embarked on my bloodstained road, I felt an obligation to continue. Because three young men dared to conspire against me, I had to attack. Douglas received notes and a warning bullet. Martin's note was illustrated by a melted dummy's head, and Tim was almost called upon to forfeit his legs. It was brutal, but they hounded me.

My conscience finally awoke with the attempt to kill Bruce Evanson. It had come to this? I had stooped to murder an attorney, a fellow member of my once-sacred profession? At last I saw my obsession for the murderous disease it was.

There is no hope to correct my crimes. I can only separate myself from you, and beg you to consider the many years that my hands were unbloodied and my service to others was commendable.

Elston Grant

When Tim completed his reading, he scouted the sheriff's reaction. "*What* is bloodrampancy?"

Kruger shrugged. "A ten-dollar word for violence, I suppose. You know how lawyers like to play with fancy terms."

"I'm learning. This is all typed...even his name. You're accepting it as genuine?"

"He shot himself at the typewriter. The gun he used matches the one that killed Sid Burk. What more do I need...a videotape of each murder, with an affidavit from the cameraman?"

Tim sat down and ran his hand over his face. "From what I've seen, it's over. We all had suspicions. None of us had a bit of proof."

Nagle shifted from one leg to the other. "You did a good job, Tim. You set out to clear your uncle, and that's happened."

"Sure. It happened by itself. I stood by and watched."

143

"You were putting pressure on him," Martin added. "In a perverse sort of way, our combined pressure stopped the killer."

For several moments, no one spoke. Then Kruger asked, "You know anything about a rifle in your uncle's car?"

"What are you suggesting---that if I found an incriminating weapon in my uncle's car, that I would deliberately hide it from *you*?"

"I'm only asking a question."

"A pointless one. You seem to be inundated with evidence that Elston Grant, and Grant alone, killed Sid Burk, his mother, and Shawn."

"So it would seem. But..."

"May I have a copy of this death note? You wouldn't have any objection to that, would you?"

"I can't think of any. But now it wouldn't be anything more than collecting a piece of memorabilia."

"Let's just say I like to collect suicide notes."

"Take that copy. But before you ask, we checked for powder burns and other fingerprints. Everything is consistent with suicide."

"Okay. If it's suicide, it's suicide." Tim stood up. "Where's Doug?"

"The last I heard, he was over at their law office, here in town. Guess he's taking it hard."

"I think I should go see him. We...we sort of worked together on trying to find the killer."

"Be my guest."

As they left, Tim and Martin shook hands with the sheriff and his chief deputy. There was a tone of conclusiveness to their parting; it was beginning to sink in that a prolonged and emotionally draining experience was, with Grant's death, officially closed.

The young investigators stepped quietly into Elston Grant's Greenharbor office. His secretary was there, stoic and poised. Thelma looked up from her typewriter.

"We had to stop by."

"Yes. I understand."

"Martin and I are very sorry about your employer's death."

"Nothing is forever, Dr. Whinney. Not my job, not this law practice. Too bad it wasn't a partnership with twenty partners, huh?"

"Have the phone calls started pouring in?"

"Only three. All out-of-town. Folks here don't ask about suicide. They'd rather hear the details from a neighbor."

"We...we wanted to talk with Doug. If he's here."

"Yes, he's here. I doubt he wants any visitors.

But I'll check."

Doug was willing to see them. Tim and Martin took chairs across from the young paralegal's desk. He looked pallid and shaken.

"A lot of wrapping up to do." Doug pulled out his checkbook. "I should pay you, Tim, to finish our little research project."

"Doug, you don't have to..."

"No, it's all right. I've got the money, and more coming, with my uncle's death. Funny thing, isn't it...how profitable death can be?" He wrote a check for two hundred dollars, and handed it to Tim. "You were right. My uncle was the best suspect. I wish you'd been wrong." Doug wiped a tear away from his eye. "He wasn't all bad, you know. He really wasn't."

"Doug, I didn't come for money. I came to see if I could help you, or do *anything* that would make it easier."

"No. No, there isn't." Doug held a handkerchief to his eyes for a few moments, then lowered it and looked composed. I always do that, don't I? Push people away. Afraid to let anyone get near me. Tim, Martin...thank you for doing what we needed to do." He came to his feet. "The past is past. I'm ready for a vacation---a change of scenery. Maybe something new...I'd like to sail a boat off the Florida coast...to swim and get tan. You guys want to go with me?"

Martin shrugged. "Maybe we *all* need a vacation."

* * *

Tim picked up a paper sack and turned out the last light in the Whinney house. Martin was at work and Tim's uncle and aunt had accompanied some friends to a pre-Independence Day festivity. The bright moon, the dark house and the warm July night all blended into a nocturnal panoply as Tim slipped out the front door and drove to the Flinn farm to pick up Lisa.

Tim took Lisa to the county park on the north edge of Greenharbor. Other than an exuberant ballgame at the baseball diamond, the park had few patrons.

"They're waiting for tomorrow," Lisa remarked as she and Tim skirted around the sports enthusiasts. "Fireworks, the town band...this place will be roaring from noon on."

With his right hand Tim clasped Lisa's fingers, and with his left hand he held the small sack. "I'm glad we've got moonlight. We've never hiked up this trail in the dark before, have we?"

"No, I think we've always gone in the daytime. But

except for a few stray branches, it should be perfectly safe. Would you mind carrying this blanket?"

"Oh...sure...somehow I hadn't noticed the blanket."

"You'd certainly have noticed not having it when we got to the clearing."

They pressed on through the shaded darkness, with the tree limbs obscuring the moon. Several minutes later their circuitous path ended as it opened into the oval-shaped clearing halfway up King's Hill.

Tim stretched out on the blanket, resting his back against a tall maple tree. Lisa sat next to him, and her face was more clearly visible after a small cloud passed by and moonlight streamed into the clearing.

"I believe we're here to discuss college and future plans and ships that pass in the night."

"All of that, if you wish." Tim folded his arms. "But I'd like to talk about the two of us. Is it okay if I ramble for a minute or two?"

"Go ahead."

"Lisa, I think I loved you from the first moment I saw you. At the very least, I had brains enough to realize you had a beautiful face and a beautiful body. As we dated, it became quite clear that your personality and your character were carved from the same precious stone. I never thought it would work between us, because of money and miles and my deep-seated fear that you'd wake up to what a slim catch I'd make for anybody. But you saved my life, you captured my imagination, you won my heart, and for once in my life I'm going to be a high-roller. So, with that in mind, I want to give you something."

Tim produced a tiny pink box in his right hand. He opened it and the gold ring inside sparkled in the beam of his flashlight.

"Please permit me a brief description." Tim held the ring between his finger and thumb, where they could both see it. "The two center gems were cut so that they form a yin and yang pattern. The sky blue on top is chalcedony for your birth month, and the dark blue sapphire represents my birth month. The four engraved roses that border the gems will have a fiery sparkle in the sunlight. That's because the jeweler who made this inlaid miniature chips of ruby to form the rose petals."

"Oh, Tim...it's the most gorgeous ring I've ever seen in my life."

"My suggestion is that you wave it around a lot, and then maybe people won't notice that your husband is a modestly paid university professor. Lisa...will you marry me?"

"As long as it's taken you to get to the point, I

really should keep you waiting for another month. But since there's an outside chance you could change your mind, I'll be gracious about it and say that if the ring fits, I'll marry you."

"It'll fit. Your hand, please."

She sat and stared at the ring. "I can't believe it's really happening."

"Happy Fourth of July." Tim switched off the flashlight and gave her a lingering kiss. "It would be great if roses and rings and treasure in the earth were all we had to think about. But I can't escape the haunting thought that the river is threatening us."

"The *river*?"

"Floods. Watery death. A pond turning red while I scream out Shawn's name. Crazy things to have in your head on the day you propose, don't you think?"

She put her arms around him. "You've been through so much this summer---so incredibly much. But it's over, Tim. We're free."

"I'll be honest, Lisa. I wanted to solve those murders. I wanted to hear somebody, somewhere say with just a particle of pride, 'Tim Whinney solved that case.' I didn't want to finish out of the money. But, if it had to happen, I will cheerfully admit that I've won the sweetest consolation prize in the whole world."

"Everything balances out when you've got the right accountant. Remember the saying on your coffee cup: Accountants Never Lose Their Balance."

He leaned forward and intercepted her lips with his own.

Chapter Twenty-four

After projects have been selected and funds appropriated for capital expenditures, budgetary control must be exercised to ensure monies are spent as directed and that line management is provided adequate feedback about the projects.
Greg M. Thibadoux

Early in the afternoon of the Fourth of July, Tim met with Lyda's attorney, Bruce Evanson.

"I'm surprised to find you working on a holiday," Tim said. "Are you any closer to recovering Sparlin Farm?"

Bruce frowned. "Not necessarily. The ancient president of the Martin Luther King Foundation of Greenharbor is barely able to understand that Grant died. I mean, this old guy gives new depth to the term 'advanced senility.' So it's at a standstill. They might turn to Grant's nephew...or me...or even Ling Sumoto to be the next executive director. It's up in the air, as far as I can tell."

"Did you get a copy of Grant's death note?"

"Yes I did." Bruce shuffled through some papers and located a copy of the message. "It was a 'lifelong obsession to bring a Grant estate back into existence,' huh? No wonder we never got along. If his mind was that far in the past, he must've thought I was a slave."

* * *

That night, exhausted from the busywork of planning a wedding, Tim began a sound night's sleep in his bedroom.

Then, startlingly, it began once more. The yellow candle flickered and became more brilliant. Tim saw himself in a living room chair, hearing the same vibrant words. "The search continues for Midnight. Apparently no one can find him. If you're going to join the manhunt, you'd better hurry. Hundreds of would-be detectives are on his trail." Tim saw three candles on a nearby table as he tossed a magazine aside. A sense of excitement stirred him. Perhaps he could find Midnight.

A hillside of sunswept roses, glowing like vermilion daggers, provided a transitional splash of color. Tim walked slowly but purposefully into the monastery. "We must talk about my quest," he told the monk.

"It can wait. It can be delayed. Here, have a

piece of fruit."

"No...no, I'd rather not."

"There's nothing to fear, my son. You are in a domicile dedicated to sacred deeds."

"Yes. Of course. All right, I'll try the fruit."

The fruit was tasty and satisfying.

"So, my young friend, you cannot be dissuaded?"

"It seems to me...and please don't think I'm arrogant...that I have special qualifications to find this man. Haven't I always yearned to be a solver of perplexing puzzles? Haven't I studied and trained for such work?"

"You are young, and your experience would barely fill a thimble. If you take this fork in the road, my son, you will come to know death as something close, crimson and incorrigible."

"Well...yes...that may prove true..."

Tim walked away from the monastery, noting three red roses as he traveled along the pathway.

After a moment of blackness, three bells pealed vibrantly. Tim turned to his friend. "The monk was wrong, Martin. This is something I *can* do, and should do."

"We'll swoop down on Midnight like nimble ravens," Martin returned supportively.

Soon they reached the edge of a gigantic, moss-covered mountain. "He's here, Tim. Midnight is hiding here, on the mountain. Follow me."

Tim followed, but he yearned to lead rather than trail behind. And he worried each time Martin came perilously close to the edge of the steep mountain trail. "Hold up, Martin. Slow down and rest. I'll take the lead for a bit."

Five black crows flew overhead.

Rounding a sharp turn on the jagged path, Tim stumbled into a tall, slim man in a pale green overcoat. For a moment the man's face was ancient, unearthly, ice-cold and cadaverous.

"I've seen you before," Tim exclaimed. "But I don't know you. Who are you?"

"My name is Midnight." The face changed again, reminding Tim of an eighty-year-old Adolph Hitler. A pistol slid from the raincoat to the man's hand. "Midnight means death."

Tim's heart pounded. "No! No! I can't die! I have a wife now! My history is unwritten. *Please* don't kill me!"

"But you *wanted* this, didn't you, Dr. Whinney? You *wanted* to find me. It excited you. Your desire to impregnate history with your fame was greater than your desire for a family, wasn't it? For this vain-glorious sin, you shall die!"

"No! Please! I love Lisa! Let me live!"

A shoe flashed across the image. A man's shoe and trouser leg came into focus, kicking the pistol from Midnight's hand. With a yelp of pain, the evil personification receded into the viridescent shadows and disappeared.

Wiping the sweat from his forehead, Tim turned to see who had saved his life.

The handsome figure in the dark green sweater and trousers was Shawn. Every trace of anxiety melted as Tim beheld his friend.

Tim took a step closer. "I'm not sure I understand, but...my god, it's good to see you."

Shawn hugged Tim, and extended his arm to touch Martin's shoulder. Then the rescuer pulled back.

"It's good to be here, Tim. Before you ask, no, I can't hang around and be your dream-advisor. But there's one thing you need to know. In fact, I made a special trip back to this part of the galaxy, just to tell you. Elston Grant...is not the man who killed me."

Chapter Twenty-five

Adherence to GAAP [should assure] that financial reports of all state and local governments--regardless of jurisdictional legal provisions and customs--[will] contain the same types of financial statements and disclosures, for the same categories and types of funds and account groups, based on the same measurement and classification criteria.
GAAP Codification, Sec. 1200.102

John Miller fumbled through a mountain of budget information at his desk. As city manager of Greenharbor, it was his responsibility to submit the proposed operating budget for next year to the mayor and city council within three weeks. The operating budget included the general fund and two special revenue funds, and used the traditional (line-item) approach.

George Kinney, the budget officer, walked into John's office. "What's up, John? I thought we were nearly done with the proposed budget."

"Well, there certainly is a ton of data," said John. "We have dollar amounts for every spending category of each division in all departments. There must be 10,000 numbers. But how do I explain next year's operations to the city council?"

"But John, you have a copy of the summary of operations I prepared for your budget message," replied an exasperated George. "Doesn't that explain everything?"

"Sure," said John. "We talk about our projected revenue increases that should total 12%. And our new training program for police and fire recruits. But they question everything. They'll want to know why the park's land and acquisition budget is cut 40% and police training is up 30%."

"We have the answers to all these questions; what's the problem?" exclaimed George.

"I sound like a used car salesman, George. There is nothing systematic about our budget process. Other cities use sophisticated budgeting procedures. I think it's time to do the same."

George thought about the idea momentarily. "You may be right, John. Most of the cities that use zero-based or program budgeting are larger than Greenharbor, but its worth considering. Let me review some ideas with the finance department and I'll get back to you tomorrow."

* * *

George had thought about program budgeting before. Considering each division as a separate program, with program objectives and specific performance measures, made a lot of sense. George invited Jeff Spencer, the public works director, to his office. Jeff had thought seriously about program budget procedures for his department.

"Hi Jeff. Have a seat. John wants to explore the possibility of introducing sophisticated budgeting procedures into the proposed budget. I know you've done some preliminary work on program budgeting. What's your opinion?"

Jeff didn't hesitate to respond, "Not this year. Program budgeting cannot be implemented quickly. Neither can ZBB. Think about the street repair and maintenance division. They repair potholes, keep roads clear after storms, and pave roads periodically. We can develop general guidelines and objectives. But it's difficult to be specific. And more difficult to develop performance measures. How many potholes need to be filled to meet the budget? We planned to expand Broadway to a four lane road this year, but deferred the project because of all the road damage from last winter's storms. How do we plan for all contingencies and meet budget performance measures?"

"Jeff, I thought you'd be a bit more positive."

"Long-term, I am. But the budget must be finalized in less than a month. There may be a short-term solution. Elm City uses line-item budgeting for the continuation of existing programs. They factor in inflation and population growth. Then they use ZBB for new programs. Inflation has been running three to four percent this year and salary increases will average four percent. Population growth was only two percent. So growth and inflation should account for about half the projected increase in revenues. John has mentioned only two new programs, the public safety training program and buying new computers for the finance department. Prepare decision packages on these items and add one or two more for the city council to consider and you've got a terrific budget package. Then let's plan a program budgeting proposal for next year."

"Jeff, that sounds like a great idea. I'll work up some ZBB numbers and propose it to John tomorrow."

* * *

George went to work on the capital budget ten year

projection report. This internal document was revised annually to plan capital projects and related debt service costs. In the last few years only three capital projects were started and all were completed. Of course, long-term bonds had been issued for each. The two G.O. bond issues were 20 year serial bonds, while the special assessment bonds would be paid off within six years. But things were changing. Virtually all departments had capital projects in the planning stage and the city council was hearing complaints on the inadequate infrastructure in the city. Planning and finding ways to fund these projects were going to require long days in the budget office. The projects had to be financed, built, and long-term debt serviced.

Leasing also was an option for capital equipment and other fixed assets. At present a special revenue fund was used for public safety equipment purchases. In the future, equipment would be purchased using G.O. bonds or other debt instruments rather than current revenues. This was the first priority. George had his preliminary numbers and phoned Sheriff Don Kruger to get his support.

"Don, this is George. I've got some ideas on equipment purchasing. Have you got time to go over the alternatives?"

"Sure do," said the sheriff.

"I want to return fines and forfeitures revenue back to the General Fund and purchase equipment with debt or on lease. We now have 12 police cars and we usually keep them about three years. The most logical plan is to replace a third of them annually. That way the average age of the fleet will continue to be less than two years old. We can either lease the cars for three years or buy them at low bid. If we buy, we'll have to use bank notes, because the annual cost is too low to enter the bond market. However, the interest rates on bank notes will be relatively high."

"Your plan sounds okay," responded the sheriff. "Should we lease or buy?"

"There are tradeoffs, Don. My preference is to lease. On a short-term lease the three-year payments are less than 90% of the market value on a present value basis. Therefore, it would be an operating lease. It's off-balance sheet and we don't book the debt. And the annual payments are much less than the interest and principal costs on a bank note. However, the cars are not ours to be auctioned off after three years. Auction prices have averaged about 25% of purchase price. The present value of the lease is about $200 a car lower than the purchase, but there's less hassle and the cash flows are regular."

"Do you really think Sally will agree to the higher present value?" laughed Sheriff Kruger. "If you want the lease you'd better negotiate a lower price."

"You're probably right, Don. But if she wants the purchase approach, she'll have to help to solve the cash flow headaches. Thanks for your advice. I'll call Sally and John and see if we can reach a decision. See you later."

George called Sally, John, and Paul McDaniel, the fire chief The situation was similar for fire equipment. Sheriff Kruger was right; Sally insisted on the lower present value of the purchase and John approved the plan. One decision made, thought George. Solve a half dozen more and I can go to lunch.

Chapter Twenty-Six

The computer allows the entity to efficiently store voluminous data. It also allows the use of sophisticated budgeting models. In short, the computer dramatically increases the effectiveness of budgets. With proper implementation, a computerized budget can generate more and better information, assist in insightful analyses, and eventually help management cope with the ever-increasing dynamic environment that all governments face.

W. Ken Harmon
Kay M. Poston

"It ended there," Tim told Martin as they had breakfast together the next morning. "I was *so* frightened, so sure that I'd go through the dying experience again...but then it spun around. In reality, I couldn't save Shawn. In the dream, he saved me."

"There's no excuse for that dream coming back," Martin said firmly. "It should be completely behind you now."

"I didn't mind." Tim finished another spoonful of raisin bran. "Shawn looked great."

"Come on, Tim, Shawn is dead! These dreams have got to stop. I've got the name of a lady in Cleveland who handles things like this--makes bad dreams go away---and I'm calling her. I'm setting up an appointment."

"Martin, I think that dream had a purpose. Now whether it was actually Shawn visiting, my subconscious mind, or an intuitive energy beam, I don't know. Let the theologians wrangle. But I got the message. Elston Grant didn't kill Shawn, and I've got growing doubts that he killed anyone."

"Tim, you'll make a fool of yourself. The case is closed, Grant did it, and a nutty dream changes nothing."

* * *

As lunchtime approached, Tim made another trip into Greenharbor to place the order for wedding invitations. On Connecticut Street Tim bumped into Deputy Nagle.

"What's on your mind, Deputy?"

"Just idle thoughts." Nagle cleared his throat. "Still in all, I wouldn't object to hearing your reaction. You had lunch yet?"

Tim glanced at his watch. "No, but I see it's time."

"I'll buy you a hamburger at the place across the

street."

Once seated in their booth, Nagle placed an order, scanned the nearby booths for untrustworthy listeners, and finally began his uncharacteristically softspoken comments.

"The fact that the suicide note was typed is beginning to bother me. At first, I thought maybe this guy always typed things, and it was like a pianist casually sitting down at the keyboard. But then I talked to his secretary. She says he hated to type, and gave her everything in longhand or on a cassette. So I asked myself, 'Why'd he type that note?'"

Tim waited until their soft drinks arrived. "I'm not arguing, and I've got similar suspicions. But let me play devil's advocate. Perhaps this was an extremely important message for him---his freedom from spirit-strangling guilt. If so, he couldn't afford to have it misunderstood or misread. So he typed it. Isn't that possible?"

"Sure...but it seems odd."

They waited for the hamburgers to be placed on the table. Tim ate and Nagle pressed on.

"Another thing...this Grant estate that his dear grandfather loved so much, with music from *Gone with the Wind* playing in the background. I did some checking. Sure, his grandfather owned about three hundred acres, west of here where it's a lot flatter. But the old man rented out the land and never farmed it or bothered with it. Furthermore, Grant was no pauper and I've found three different people who offered to sell him farmland at reasonable prices, over the last ten years. Grant told them all no thanks and kept his money in tax-free government bonds. How does any of that support a 'lifelong obsession' to preside over a country estate?"

"Hmmm. You raise a good point."

Novia Dixon was almost past them when she noticed Tim. "Oh...Professor Whinney."

"Better known as Tim." He smiled.

"Of course. Tim. Now maybe we can all get back to first names and being less suspicious. It's such a relief."

"So it would appear. Novia, have you met Chief Deputy Nagle?"

"Why...I'm not sure...oh, the inquest..."

Nagle stood up and nervously shook the theater director's hand. "A pleasure, Miss Dixon. I really enjoy those plays...about the best entertainment we get, here in Greenharbor. Oh that Greek one was a little strange...but I was there. Didn't want the box office to suffer just because you were brave enough to try

156

something new and expressive."

"Why thank you, Deputy Nagle. I've got to run, gentlemen. Important meeting with Mr. Sumoto. So good to see you."

Nagle and Tim settled back into their seats. The younger man swallowed a sip of Coke. "Now there's one lady who's just too pretty to be a good suspect, even if she'd been there at the exact time Burk died."

"You're right."

"Or at least, I think she's pretty. What do you think, Deputy?"

"Closer to beautiful, in my opinion. Can't understand for one minute why she's single."

"Maybe all the guys who do the wondering are too busy thinking about it to ask her for a date. Why don't you ask her out?"

"Me?" Nagle snickered. "She wouldn't go out with me."

"I'd give it a try. Martin tells me she doesn't get asked out nearly as often as she'd like."

"You don't say." Nagle nibbled some fries. "I think the murderer could still be running around loose. How crazy does that sound to you?"

"Not crazy at all, deputy. Not crazy at all."

* * *

At one o'clock, Tim noticed Martin's convertible in the parking area that was immediately north of Mr. Sumoto's office. Tim stepped inside the building and soon located his friend.

Martin looked up from the report he was preparing. "I went ahead and made the appointment with the lady from Cleveland who explains dreams. She'll be in Greenharbor this coming Monday. But you don't have to see her if you don't want to." His tone was soft and conciliatory. "I guess you know that."

Tim nodded. "I hope the day never comes when I'll be unwilling to consider my best friend's advice. Yes, I want to see her. I'd like to get rid of Midnight forever."

"Good. And by the way, I meant to tell you what a masterful job you did in answering the sheriff's question about that planted rifle."

Tim smiled weakly. "We've got to stay friends. If you ever tell everything you know about me, I'll hang."

"It cuts both ways. You know most of my secrets. Incidentally, the lab didn't find any prints on the rifle. But if we could check the markings, it might prove to be the rifle that killed Shawn." Martin sat on the edge of the desk, folding his right leg and holding his ankle. "You've lost your faith that Grant was the killer, haven't you?"

Tim stretched his fingers as if reaching for an invisible object. "Call me an atheist."

"If you're right, it means two things. Number one, the real killer is still crawling around, and could strike in a minute if our suspicions surfaced. Number two, the job's twice as tough. Nobody wants to go back to all that tension. Since this morning, I've taken the idea that maybe Grant was murdered and framed, and I've flown it by three people. They've all politely responded, 'You're crazy; forget it.' They don't want to hear it. They'd rather see a man of dubious guilt tried and executed---they prefer that to the strain of having a murderer certified as being at large."

"Ordinary people like to believe convenient fairy tales. But we're different."

"I suppose." Martin got up and walked to the window. "Tilting at windmills, chasing great white whales..."

"There's never a dull moment when you and I are on the job," Tim concluded.

Martin turned off the light. "You want to go with me? I've got to pick up Doreen because her car's in the shop."

"You mean Susi Sumoto's assistant manager? Sure, I'll ride along."

The Zippa convertible backed into the alley from its parking bay. Because a pickup truck was coming in from Massachusetts Street, Martin had to wait a few moments. Taking advantage of the delay, he lowered his convertible top. "Might as well catch some rays."

"Good day for it."

The pickup cleared the narrow alley and pulled into a space next to the one Martin's car had occupied. A handsome, dark-haired youth emerged from the truck and waved at Martin, who returned the greeting.

"That's Bill. Runs the paint store on the west side of us."

With Bill now out of the way and unloading some paint, Martin eased his Chrysler onto Massachusetts and turned right. The street soon turned into Massachusetts Road as it knifed through the tall hills, meandering its way toward State Route 800.

"I'm going to miss all of this," Martin said over the road and wind noise. "Giant hills, twisty roads, dead bodies, melted mannequins in pizza ovens..."

"You're the one who predicted that the big event of the summer would be buying chickens."

"I guessed wrong."

Two miles to the west, the hills briefly gave way to an elongated valley. Martin turned right and drove northward on a gravel lane. "This is an isolated little farm that Doreen and her parents own. There's steep hills all around and a stream in front of the house."

As Martin's car rolled closer to the three-feet-deep streambed, a wooden drawbridge came down and permitted the vehicle to cross the water.

"How about that...she saw us coming," Tim surmised.

Martin stopped in front of the farmhouse and waited for Doreen to appear. Tim and his comrade discussed several subjects including the government audit as the minutes ticked away. Finally Tim peeked at his watch. Doreen *had* to see us, didn't she? She let the ramp-deal down."

"I think 'drawbridge' is the proper term. Yes, she ought to be coming. I'll give the horn a try."

Twenty seconds later Doreen's head appeared at a window. "You guys here?"

"Ready and waiting."

Doreen hustled on out to the car. Tim decided to be courteous and hopped into the back seat. "Take the front, my good lady. We thought you saw us 'cause you let the drawbridge down."

"Oh, that gizmo's automatic. A wire trips it when you're driving up."

"Is that right?" Tim gave the matter some thought as they turned around and headed back to Greenharbor. "A trip-wire. One person could use it unaided...hmmm...that reminds me of...not 'teaming up'...the danger of it...but with a..."

"What's all the mumbling about, Tim?"

"I just figured out how something could've been done...that would answer a puzzling question...that explains the parking...and the reason, the real reason for the trip...give me another minute to think this through."

"You go right ahead, Tim. Doreen and I would never think of imposing on your incoherent thought patterns, would we, Doreen?"

"Absolutely not."

But the images in Tim's mind were far more precise than his jumbled speech suggested. A dark pattern of scattered triangles began to self-assemble. Dry bones began to assume flesh, and buried words broke through the sand. Bridges...connections...a flurry of images crowded into Tim's mind. Doreen's bridge that connected her wilderness outpost with civilization. The rake at the crematory, that connected the living and the dead.

The dream that connected Shawn's new world with life on earth.

Tim leaned forward and put his hand on Martin's shoulder. "I know who the murderer is."

Doreen turned to her left. "Are you talking about that killer? Elston Grant?"

"Elston Grant was a victim. He killed no one," Tim said.

As they came into view of Greenharbor Martin said, "I'm all ears, Tim. Who?"

"Give me a day or two, so I can think, rethink, triplethink ...check all the evidence. If I'm right, careful testing can only confirm it."

Martin slowed down and flipped on his left-turn signal. "Fine. Think and test to your heart's content. But let me give you some very serious advice. *Keep it quiet.* If the killer suspects that you're pursuing him...chasing Midnight along that deadly mountain trail...then the killer could decide to arrange a fatal accident. You've got Lisa to think about..."

At that moment, with Martin's car less than a block away from the Pasta Superba, the street quaked and shimmied as a tremendous blast of debris erupted from the paint store and the Pasta Superba. Several buckets of paint flew into the air, then crashed heavily as the entire front wall of the paint store disintegrated.

Martin skidded to a halt and gazed unbelievingly at the chaos. "Oh my god. Bill's inside that store."

Chapter Twenty-seven

Effective and efficient cash and investment management is a prerequisite to maintaining control over fiscal matters.
                              Judith K. Welch
                              J. Dwight Hadley

After a moment of numbing shock, Tim and Martin leaped out of the convertible and raced through paint cans, dust, broken glass and bricks to see if any occupants could be rescued. One young man with dark hair and a slim build had just left the paint store, and the force of the blast had knocked him down. Two passersby helped him to his feet.

Fighting their way into the interior of the wrecked building, the duo found Bill lying on the floor near a counter. The paint store manager was conscious, and touched his hand to his black hair. "I...think...there may not be much of my...head left."

Martin endeavored to make him comfortable. "You're fine...you're all in one piece. Just take it easy until an ambulance gets here."

In short order, an ambulance arrived and Bill was taken to Greenharbor's small hospital. The young man outside appeared uninjured and declined any treatment. No other victims were located.

"Could've been worse," Martin theorized. "Could've killed half a dozen people."

"You can say that again. The Pasta Superba will need some repairs. The authorities might not want it to open anyway, until it's clear what caused the explosion."

"I'm keenly eager to hear the verdict," Tim replied.

Everyone was obliged to wait until five p.m., when Sheriff Kruger stepped in front of a group of spectators and made a short statement for the public record. "I've conferred with the fire chief, and our best guess at this point is that a natural gas leak was the cause of the accident. An old pipe gave way near the rear of the Italian restaurant, but for some reason most of the gas was directed to the paint store. We'll put that in fancier words and make an official statement tomorrow morning."

Their curiosity seemingly satisfied, most of the onlookers began to disperse. Before long, only Tim and Martin were standing in the shaded doorway of the Pasta Superba. For safety reasons, the power to the building remained off.

"If we'd gotten here two minutes quicker, we could've been killed," Martin said.

"Distinctly possible," Tim agreed. "Thank goodness Doreen was in no hurry to come out to the car."

"I smell a rat. Yeah, looks like an accident, *sure*. But spin the propeller in the opposite direction, and see what you've got. With Bill's black hair and suntan---plus we both run around in white clothes a lot of the time---somebody at a distance could confuse him for me. The guy on the street---his customer---looked a lot like you. Some nervous triggerman could've made a mistake...leaving us adrift in a lifeboat until the next accidental raid can destroy us."

"You may be right. I've tried to tell only a few people that I believe Elston Grant's death was a cover-up. Still, word could get out...and quite possibly the killer senses that our presence is an ongoing threat."

"Tim...you can't leave Lisa at school...walking around on that campus, going places at night...never suspecting that she's a target if you're a target."

Tim considered his friend's comments for several moments. "Okay. We're getting close to the killer's identity...and the killer is getting desperate. No more sitting ducks...no more Shawns...you're right. You and Lisa and me...we need seclusion. We need to become very hard to find."

"Then let's do it. Let's go and collect Lisa, and let's start being invisible unless we've got somebody to interview."

* * *

On Thursday morning, Lisa returned to Greenharbor with Tim and Martin. Explanations were given, and a deadline was set.

"Monday," Tim told his uncle and aunt. "If Mrs. Wright arrives on schedule, my recurring dream gets explained then."

"*What* dream?"

"I'll tell you all about it, as soon as that's practical. But more importantly, I'm putting the gears in motion to bring this whole diabolical mess to a conclusion...Monday."

Tim and Martin packed their bags and drove to the Flinn farm, where Lyda had sensed the rightness of their plan, and had helped Lisa pack a few belongings.

The Flinns were upset and confused. Lisa's parents found it difficult to separate the concepts of elopement and protective seclusion.

"*Why is this necessary*?" was the key question.

Tim took a deep breath and started talking. He knew his explanation had to make sense, or his marriage would be clouded by some heavy parental hostility. "Four murders make it necessary. Sid Burk was murdered. You know that. His mother was also murdered. That would be harder to prove, if it weren't for Elston Grant's death note. Even though the suicide message was a lie, the murderer made the ruse more credible by conceding the second murder. Shawn Sparlin was murdered. Mr. and Mrs. Flinn, you're upset with me, and you'd like to paint a picture of a reckless young man who doesn't have a ghost of an idea what he's doing. Well let me remind you of something. When Shawn Sparlin was shot, I was sitting closer to him than I am to you. I held him in my arms as he took his last gasp of breath. Yeah, I'm an accountant and not a cop, but I know *exactly* what I'm doing. I'm seeing to it that Shawn's murderer goes to prison and stays there. To reach that goal, I need evidence, I need assistance in getting the evidence, and I need to keep the potential victims of *accidental* gas explosions from getting killed."

Tim's words apparently had some effect, because the chorus of objections turned into deafening silence. To break the stalemate, Lyda spoke up. "If you've got doubts about the wisdom of Tim's plan, why don't you telephone an attorney? Bruce Evanson knows what's going on. He'll give you an honest opinion."

This suggestion was accepted and Bruce Evanson voiced confidence in Tim's approach. To allay parental concern, Bruce promised that he would be in continual contact with Tim and Lisa, and provide legal guidance as the flow of events moved toward Monday.

"If I might be permitted one brief word in all of this," Lisa said with a dictatorial smile, "I'm past the age of legal adulthood, I'm not a baby, and I prefer to share this burden with the man I'm going to marry."

With such sentiments, the tide turned, and before long the three wandering detectives were seeking the open road in Martin's convertible. But---one small problem remained. Where could they hide? Where could they settle in, assured that a cunning adversary would *never* think to search for them there?

* * *

"This is about the most *unbalanced*, idiotic thing I've ever done," Nagle griped as he threw a pair of socks into his suitcase. "Letting three bloodhounds chase me out of my own home." He shook a bouncing finger at Tim. "You are taking advantage of my kindhearted nature!"

"I plead guilty. But please remember the terms of our agreement. In return for your gracious hospitality, I will keep you and Bruce updated on my research and conclusions. I believe I know the killer's identity. Right or wrong, I'll share my thoughts with you on Saturday. You'll be *in the know*, Deputy. You'll establish yourself as a *leader*."

"Well...just don't throw any wild parties."

"We'll be too busy for that. Good-by, and enjoy the motel room that Bruce is generously renting for you."

By Thursday night, the three teammates were comfortably established in Nagle's small cottage, one mile west of Greenharbor. Tim gathered his two close allies around the living room coffee table, a pile of papers in hand. "Lisa, while you and Martin were buying some groceries for us at the store, I went over the trail of paper one more time. I'm glad that I've been meticulous about keeping copies of letters, notes and speeches. I needed some objective evidence that my intuitive hunch was correct...and you can tell who really wrote Elston Grant's death note. That writer, of course, is the murderer."

Accepting the challenge, first Lisa and then Martin read the pieces of evidence line by line, probingly and painstakingly. Tim had made a small wager with himself that Martin would see it first, not because he was smarter---perhaps he was, perhaps he wasn't---but because he was a grammarian, and because he had had more experience reading the Internal Revenue Code.

A flicker of light crossed Martin's face. "Style."

"Bingo," Tim confirmed.

"I'm sorry," Lisa sighed as she put the papers aside, "but these papers don't reveal anyone as the murderer."

"In a sense, they do. In a grammatical or word-choice sense, they do."

* * *

After a succulent spaghetti dinner, and three more hours of planning, the trio retired for their first night in Nagle's two-bedroom house. Martin was odd-man-out and took the couch.

As the hour of midnight approached, Tim again experienced the candle, the monk, the ill-boding crows, and the sneering hatred of Midnight.

Suddenly, Tim was awake. "Stupid dream," he muttered.

* * *

Dream or no dream, the days were pressing in, and Tim knew that acting quickly was an essential ingredient for resolving the murders. Borrowing Nagle's house had bought them only a small amount of time.

With these thoughts in mind, Tim conducted the first of five final interviews. The original six possibilities were now the surviving five, and one of them was a deadly killer.

"Mr. Sumoto, for the last time, I'd like to get it straight. Did Sid Burk raise the price on you, or did he not raise the price?"

Ling Sumoto sipped some tea. "At that point, I did not have the owner's name. Mrs. Barger gave me a sliding scale of acreage cost. When I indicated that I might well agree to exchange the land, she checked with someone---I now presume it was Burk---and the price went right up to the top dollar. I was suspicious. It made me feel...what is the slang term...like a sucker. But I was not enraged."

"Nonetheless, I'm sure you appreciate how circumstances can incriminate. You were seen in the Pasta Superba only minutes before that mannequin head frightened Doreen. You were out of town the weekend I was attacked in Cortino. If anybody were to fake a gas explosion, you would have the most familiarity with the old pipes in a building you own."

"Yes, I see where suspicion might surface. But how many votes to convict would such weak evidence engender? Two votes out of twelve? Three? I leave that to your contemplation."

* * *

Martin had the assignment of interviewing Verna Barger. As usual, the real estate broker sat at her desk with her jet black hair raked into a bun, and the merest touch of white face powder lightening a pale complexion.

"It's a small town, Mr. Zippa. You and Professor Whinney had better catch this killer before he wipes us off the map."

Martin smiled. "That's our goal, and you can help us reach it. First, would it be true that you frequently write descriptions of property, information on land, and so forth?"

"Yes. That would be true."

"Could I get from you a couple of samples of your

prose?"

"I suppose so, but I have serious doubts as to how many killers that will catch. Oh. You probably want my description of Orick Farm, don't you?"

"That would be fine."

Mrs. Barger plowed through a stack of papers on another desk, and eventually came up with some paperwork on Orick Farm. "Here you are. Free of charge, I'm throwing in three ads that I wrote recently."

"Thanks." Martin accepted the papers. "I'll photocopy them and return the originals. Now, to deal with rumors. On the twenty-third of June, you had a phone conversation with somebody, quite possibly Elston Grant. Our witness heard only part of the conversation, but you apparently told Mr. Grant that he would draw less suspicion if he sold some property through you. Could you confirm that the reference was to the three adjacent properties he then owned?"

"Just one question, Mr. Zippa. How many drinks did your witness have before hearing this twittery conversation?"

"Probably none. Did you talk to Grant that day?"

"I hardly ever talked to the man. Here, let's check my phone log." She perused a large, flat notebook. "In my business, you keep track of people, prices and properties. What was that date?"

"June twenty-three."

"On...that day, I...oh, for crying in the soda water..." Her finger came to a stop. "That wasn't Elston Grant, it was Elmer Smith!"

"Who?"

"Smith, the tight-fisted farmer out on New Jersey Road. Dentures don't fit. I helped him sell some land back to his brother-in-law. Sapheaded family feud. That's who your rabbit-eared witness heard me talking to."

"Oh," Martin answered.

* * *

Lisa interviewed Novia Dixon, to get the theater director's final thoughts on the murders. "While I'm here, Miss Dixon,. I understand that you wrote some publicity materials on the plays you direct. Handouts for the newspapers. Would you object if I took a copy?"

"Not at all. I'll go back to the files and get you one. Oh...by the way...I've been trying to get in touch with Martin, but he seems to have almost disappeared. Do you know if he's in town?"

"I think so. I see more of him during the late

evening hours."

"Perhaps I could give you a note...and ask you to pass it on to him?"

"Certainly." Lisa waited patiently until Novia returned with two press releases and a sealed envelope.

"On a change of subject, Miss Dixon---do you fire a rifle very often?"

Novia raised her eyebrows in an animated expression of surprise. "Are you kidding? Our toy prop guns make me nervous. I have *nothing* to do with guns." She returned to her chair. "If you want to talk to a female expert on firearms, I suggest you speak to Verna Barger. She often bragged about how good she was with a gun...back in the days when Elston Grant, Shawn Sparlin and Sid Burk were all alive, and it was not indelicate to discuss such things."

* * *

Tim visited with Walter and Grace Rankin in their Greenharbor motel room.

"Good news about Bill, the paint store boy," Mr. Rankin reported. "His recovery is coming along smoothly."

"That's great," Tim said. After a moment of silence, he drew in a deep breath. "Do either of you have anything here that would serve as a sample of your writing?"

"Just about everything I've written is back in Cincinnati," Walter Rankin replied to Tim's query. "Well...hold on...I do just happen to have with me an article I wrote about the Wabash Cannonball."

"Precisely what we need."

"I can supply one of my poems," volunteered Grace Rankin. "Unless I'm not in this select group of contributors."

"We don't need something in writing," Tim told her, "but I recall that you've done a little acting. I have a part for you---an important part---but I must admit that there's some danger involved."

"I keep danger in my kitchen cabinet, next to the paprika," retorted Mrs. Rankin. "It's a spice that makes living more savory. What's my role?"

* * *

Returning to Novia's private office at the Greenharbor Little Theater, Martin sat on one edge of her desk.

"Yeah, it'll take courage to do it. I agree. But

not doing it... inflicts a pain of its own."
"I have things I need to do...places to go..."
"Novia...please...for me..."
"All right. At the very least, maybe I can keep *you* from getting hurt."
"Thanks." He leaned closer to her and kissed her.

* * *

Douglas Grant returned to Greenharbor after a long day's toil at the Woodsfield law firm where he worked part-time. As planned, he met with Tim and Martin at Elston Grant's Greenharbor office.
"Not much left of this place," Doug said as he made a sweeping gesture with his right arm. "The books are in boxes, the clients are scheduled to receive good-luck-finding-an-attorney letters...and the landlord kicks us out at the end of July. Poor Thelma...she'll have to hunt for a new job."
"Do you ever wish you'd gone ahead and gotten your own law degree?" Martin asked.
"Oh, you bet I wish that I had gotten it. Had the money been there..." He plopped wearily into a padded chair. "I'm bushed. I need to get away. Want to go sailing with me...the coast? I could still get a deeper tan than either of you...especially if you stayed below deck to do the work, and I caught all the sun. Shall we?"
"Other problems permitting, Martin and I like the idea. But we've got one last crisis to defuse." Tim sat down in the chair next to Doug's. "There's a murderer at large, and to stop that person...we need your help. May we count on you?"
"I'll help in any way I can, Tim. What do..."
The door to the office swung open, and in marched Deputy Nagle.
"So this is where you two are loafing. I thought we had a meeting."
"Well, we were getting around to it," Tim said. "We've got a little trip we've been talking over with Doug...and some other things..."
"You might as well take a *long, long* trip, because this murder business has been taken care of. While you amateurs have been goofing off, the sheriff's department has gotten the work done. Less than an hour ago, Sheriff Kruger took Novia Dixon into custody. It seems there may have been four murders in all...and she knows plenty about all four of them."

Chapter Twenty-eight

Various tools can be useful to government officials in cost evaluation decisions. These include cost allocation, cost-volume analysis, flexible budgeting, standard costing, and variance analysis. These tools can assist the decision maker in determining the cost of a service activity. Knowledge of service costs is necessary for effective management of government programs.
Robert W. Ingram

On Monday morning Tim and Martin returned to the Whinney farmhouse. It was the tenth of July, and it was beginning as a warm, fragrant summer day. But clouds were gathering, and afternoon rain was considered possible. Tim was relaxed, and he wanted his visit with Mrs. Wright to have as little tension as possible. Nonetheless, a discriminating eye could find signs of the volatile atmosphere that was rapidly reaching a climax. One such sign was the unmarked sheriff's cruiser that was parked near the house.

As they all sat down, Martin asked, "Did we get you enough information on the phone? We tried to cover every detail."

"I believe there's enough here for me to give you some guidance." Mrs. Wright shuffled through her notes. "Let's jump right into it. The dream, as you explained on the phone, has three parts, and demonstrably the number three dominates the dream. In such a context, the number three means the birth of new things.

"Part One is dominated by the color yellow, and a candle. Yellow refers to the intellect, or seeking knowledge. A candle means an investigation.

"In Part Two, red is an emotional color, and here seems related to blood and violence. The rose element is tricky, because the rose as a symbol can have at least eight meanings. The roses at the monastery symbolize peace. The concept of peace is jarringly disturbed by the task ahead of you, just as the monk is jarringly critical of your plans. The fruit symbolizes wisdom which you will need."

Martin interjected, "And white of course is purity."

"No, not in this case. White often means evil posing as good. The monk is trying to give Tim the wisdom to decipher evil, which is hiding behind a pretense of innocence." Mrs. Wright glanced at her notes again. "The three red roses symbolize the courage to overcome violence.

"In Part Three, black is the color of death, and the jaundiced green connotes something spoiled, rancid or diseased. A bell is a Buddhist symbol for the law. Here I see three vibrant vanguards of the law---Tim and two helpers---struggling against a dark force.

"A mountain often symbolizes a test of faith or a test of courage. The strange green color is akin to mental vibrations coming from the evil man---and perhaps one can add, coming from a diseased mind. His overcoat simply emphasizes the disguise factor. Would you agree that the green is most intense when the man comes into view?"

"Yes..." Tim agreed. "That's about right."

"I'm afraid there's no getting around five black crows as five deaths."

Martin asked, "Are the birds crows or ravens?"

"Does it matter?" Tim glanced from his friend to Mrs. Wright. "Aren't they the same kind of bird?"

"Yes, they are related, but not identical. The crow, often associated with thievery or death, presents the blended symbol of stolen lives. The larger raven, a more respected ruler of the air, carries an Apollonian aura of daring pursuit and heroic rescue."

"Oh. Well, given those definitions, I think the birds in my dream were crows. I feel a slight chill whenever I see them."

"What this man says..." Mrs. Wright noted. "His 'Midnight means death' phrase. Isn't it fascinating how often symbols insist on explaining themselves?"

"What does all the blood at the end mean?"

"As for the ending, let me suggest a more positive interpretation. You feel this part very intensely, Tim, and let's not forget that your feeling-mode is sympathetic. You may be identifying with the victims of violence, rather than foreseeing your own death."

"The fact that he's dreamed it twelve times?"

"Twelve means a complete cycle. It means...this dangerous situation is almost over."

Tim looked away from the table and gazed northward, in the direction of Sid Burk's house. "Five crows...five predicted deaths...and four known victims. It *could* be brighter, couldn't it?"

Mrs. Wright stood up. "You have my prayers. Please be careful in all your endeavors."

Tim and Martin walked her to her car. "You've been very helpful," Tim told her. "I feel as if I have that dream in my control now. You said you never asked for money...but couldn't I give you something?"

"No, Tim. What I have is a gift. I cannot take

that gift and sell it. Your future success will be my payment. Write me and let me know how things worked out."

With Mrs. Wright on her way, Tim hurriedly made final preparations for the eleven o'clock showdown.

At eleven o'clock sharp, Sheriff Kruger entered the lounge of the county law enforcement building and spoke to the small group of invited participants. "Why don't we all move to the central conference room? I'm sure that each of you will want to try out our new metal detector. It does wonders for reducing the presence of unwanted guns."

Three minutes later, the unarmed group found that the folding metal chairs in their meeting room bore small handlettered tags with the name of each guest. Nine of the twelve chairs were taken by Ling Sumoto, Lyda Sparlin, Bruce Evanson, Douglas Grant, Verna Barger, Lisa Flinn, Mildred Whinney, Everett Whinney and Walter Rankin. At the front of the room a stout oak table was flanked by smaller ones at both corners of the chamber's anterior. The sheriff stood in front of the main table, with Martin Zippa and Deputy Nagle seated at the table to the sheriff's left.

"Goodness, folks, you sure have kept the phone lines humming with questions about Novia Dixon and why she's in custody. It's just possible that we may get an answer or two from Miss Dixon herself. With that in mind, let's have a matron escort her in."

The door to the sheriff's right, one of four entryways to the room, swung open. All eyes were on Novia Dixon as she walked slowly if not majestically into the room and took the chair tagged for her. Less attention was paid to the uniformed matron, who stepped past Novia to sit in the empty chair next to Ling Sumoto. The matron, Grace Rankin, touched her sidearm as she glanced over her shoulder to see Douglas Grant behind her and Verna Barger to his immediate right.

With everyone else seated, the sheriff cleared his throat. "Now, folks, since I know very little about what we're going to do here today, it is with a sense of profound relief that I turn this meeting over to Dr. Tim Whinney."

Sheriff Kruger promptly sat down behind the frail stand in the dextral corner from the central oak table. All eyes followed Tim as he strode purposefully to a pivotal position in front of the main table.

"Good morning, everyone. We're here to learn the true identity of the person who murdered Sid Burk, Molly Burk, Shawn Sparlin and Elston Grant. Our starting point is Novia Dixon. From the first she has told us but one story---that she arrived on the scene after Burk had been killed, and she was totally uninvolved in his murder. Her story is the truth, and she was never at any time under arrest."

Tim paused for a rumble of hushed comments to subside. Before he could resume, Mr. Sumoto spoke up.

"I began to suspect that there was something bogus about Novia's so-called arrest when I learned that she was coaching an actor from her unlocked jail cell. But why did you do this, Professor Whinney? Why inflict such injury on an innocent woman's reputation?"

As the group awaited Tim's response, some eyes moved to Novia's back, anticipating that she might stand up and speak. Two eyes focussed on the protruding revolver that bulged outward from Grace Rankin's side.

"We did it for two reasons, Mr. Sumoto. First, from May the twenty-fifth to July the eighth, the element of surprise was on the killer's side. For one paltry weekend, I wanted to have the element of surprise working in my favor. Second, by creating the illusion that Novia Dixon would be tried for the murders, some protection was afforded to me and my associates, who've been in deadly jeopardy for the last few weeks."

"Then you're completely discounting Grant's fingerprints on the gun, and his suicide message?" Walter Rankin asked from the back row.

"Yes I am, because the fingerprints and powder burns were added after a close-range bullet killed him, and the typed death note was composed by the killer. Since that communication was by all logical standards written by the murderer, we can profit by comparing it to a letter by Elston Grant...and one other letter." Tim stepped to his left and accepted a stack of stapled papers from Martin. "Let's pass these out."

A minute later, Tim offered guidance on what to look for in the photocopied material. "Page One is a letter from Elston Grant to the parents of Shawn Sparlin. It's genuine and reflects Grant's typical writing style. Page Two is the suicide note. Page Three helps us focus on stylistic differences by refreshing our knowledge of English grammar. In particular---and my thanks to Martin for summarizing these points so succinctly on Page Three---we are concerned with infinitivism and gerundism. Martin is an expert in the complex statutes and regulations of government laws."

"Briefly, infinitivism is the tendency or preference to use the infinitive or to-plus-the-verb in one's speech. For example, by choosing 'I plan *to go* on a trip' instead of 'I plan on *going* on a trip.' We don't want to get overly technical, but let's add that people who like the sound of gerunds often prefer verb participles that end in -ing. So someone who leans to gerundism might say, 'I'm *planning* on *going* on a trip.' With that in mind, let's turn to Page Four and look at the grammatical-stylistic analysis of Grant's letter to the Sparlins, which is quite similar to other things he wrote."

There was a general shuffling of papers as the audience turned to Page Four.

"Number of infinitives used: zero. Gerunds and -ing participles: fifteen. You can see them---'writing, expressing, establishing, emphasizing, setting' etc.

"Now look at the analysis of the phony suicide note. Infinitives used: twenty-one. Look at them---'to apologize, to hurt, to devastate, to kill, to poison' etc. Gerunds: zero. There's one -ing participle: 'a warning bullet.' The difference in verbal choice for these two letters is the difference between day and night...the difference between lightning and a lightning bug.

"As most of you know, we collected and analyzed writing samples from all eight of the original group of suspects. Since the person who wrote the feigned death note had a proclivity for infinitivism, as forensic accountants we searched for that linguistic pattern in all of the writing samples. We found it in only one person's word choice. Turn with me please to Page Five. In the letter to Pelco, notice the number of infinitives used: twelve. Count them---'to write, to affirm, to be, to work, to determine, to build' and so on. Gerunds and -ing participles: zero. This is an amazing match between the suicide note and a letter you phrased, Douglas."

A tight smile flickered across Douglas Grant's face, then disappeared. "What is this, Tim? You're trying to accuse me of murder on the basis of some *grammar test*?"

"It was enough to convince me. But unfortunately for you, there's more. Do you want me to put it together for you, step by step?"

"I urge you to keep in mind the high cost of slander, and how hard these people are going to laugh, once you start to make a fool of yourself."

Tim leaned against the oak table as he kept his eyes on Douglas. "Pelco recontacted your uncle. They wanted to build a processing plant near here, but not in Greenharbor, and preferably by purchasing land from one or two individuals. Your uncle had no interest in a private land deal. You begged him to reconsider, because you smelled money.

"The only way you could get the land was in

partnership with an individual. You turned to Sid Burk. For a while, he seemed trustworthy. Then you found out that he was contacting others, such as the Shumways by mail, hoping to put it together behind your back and leave you out in the cold. You were furious, Doug. Maybe you only meant to scare him with that gun, but before you knew it, Sid Burk was dead. Worse, you'd given your name to the deputy when you entered our flood ravaged area."

Tim pointed toward Doug. "You had to divert everyone's suspicion, and my uncle was an obvious target. You moved the body, cleaned your trunk, and planted the toolbox.

"Sooner or later you found out that a sick old lady owned half the land you needed. *Then* you saw it, like a vision from hell: if she died with a revised will giving everything to your uncle, *he'd* be the suspect. When *he* committed suicide, you'd have three of the four properties you needed, a good chance to get the King Foundation to sell Sparlin Farm, plus you'd have your uncle's bonds and life insurance. All of these assets with a step-up in basis because of death, and all the appreciation in the assets would escape the federal income tax. All you had to do was see to it that no one noticed how all the prizes were headed for your lap."

"That's crazy. Jane Potter will tell you that it's crazy."

"I suspect that Jane Potter is dead and buried."

"That's a lie. You're lying. Tim...why are you doing this to me?"

"Because you're a murderer and you murdered four people. If Jane Potter is alive, *where is she*?"

"She...she's in Canada. You know that."

"If that's true, and I doubt it, then she's facing two choices: lie and get paid for it, or refuse to lie and get killed before she can testify."

"That's insane! Are you forgetting that I got threatening notes...that I was shot at with you?"

"No you weren't. You faked the note and hired Martin and me, so you could keep abreast of what we knew. A trip-wire set off a recording of a gunshot. The bullet nick was already there. That's why you parked at that odd angle in the alley---so I wouldn't see your side of the car."

"You're crazy. You're nuts. The deputies searched all over...they would've found a recorder."

"No. For the simple reason they weren't looking for one. My best guess is that you had a small, very powerful recorder in the hollow recess of a tree, maybe ten feet above the ground. The deputies searched for a gunman, not a hidden recorder.

"Remember Novia's play? It was an incomplete circle, closed only by the eye. In anticipating the expected, we missed the obvious. Just like that night I didn't want my aunt to know that I'd had a frightening dream, so I told her I yelled because I'd hit my toe. Even embellished my story with a make-believe bandage, to make it sound all nice and finished. Why, if she'd looked at my toe, she would've seen there wasn't any bandage there. But she saw what she wanted to see, and never thought twice about it. She closed the circle with her mind. The deputies did the same.

"It was *you*, Doug. Leading us on, helping us to see that it *had* to be your uncle framing my uncle. The rifle purchase form, and the rifle in the front seat. A stupid sheriff would arrest my uncle. A smarter sheriff would close in on *your* uncle. But we weren't supposed to realize that somebody was framing the framer, were we?"

"Are you going to blame me for the gas leak explosion, too?"

"Sure. Warning us off, trying to cripple me by the roller coaster so I'd be completely off your trail---that hadn't worked. But since your pretended killer was now dead, you couldn't shoot me. You had to try something like the gas-leak explosion...which wasn't as accurate as a gun."

Douglas Grant slowly stood up. "Okay, enough of this. I don't have to stay here and listen to your mouth. I'm hiring an attorney to sue you. But let me point out for everyone else's benefit that I would never have faked my uncle's suicide. Because suicide means the life insurance company won't pay the benefit. I'd have cut my own throat."

A look of genuine surprise crossed Tim's face. "Doug, the bonds and the land are worth four times the life insurance. And insurance proceeds are not taxable. What a scheme. The no-suicide clause ran five years, and he took the policy out six years ago."

"That's a lie!"

Walter Rankin stood up. "No it isn't. I checked the policy myself, as part of my own investigation. The five years are up. Suicide or not, Doug gets all the money."

Martin arose and pulled a folded document out of his sport coat. "If there's any doubt, I happen to have a copy of the policy."

Douglas made a quick sweeping motion and snatched the revolver from Grace's holster. A second later he grabbed Novia Dixon's arm and jerked her to her feet.

He pressed the gun against her head.

"Put your gun on the floor and kick it away, Kruger. You too, Nagle." As they complied, Douglas moved his hostage closer to the door near the sheriff.

"Get over there, Kruger."

As the sheriff withdrew, Tim edged further away from the gun, toward Martin's position. "Just tell me one thing, Doug. Why? Why kill Shawn? What did he ever do to you?"

"Even if he'd really owned the land, he wouldn't have sold. He wanted to keep the blasted pond! Well he got to keep it, all right. He got to die in it."

Tim took a step forward. "Doug, I'm going to have to take that gun away from you."

Douglas Grant continued to hold Novia closely as he pointed the gun at Tim. "That stupid mistake will cost you your life." Doug pulled the trigger. There was a collective gasp, but the gun only clicked.

The young gunman stared at his weapon, and his face began to register panic. He glanced at the matron.

"I'm not as stupid as I look, either," Grace informed the killer.

With animal fury, Douglas shoved Novia Dixon toward the sheriff, then whirled to run out the exit.

Tim's plan had been to station a deputy outside each of the four doors. This procedure had been done, but one of the four men was only vaguely following the intense confrontation on the other side of the door. When Douglas emerged, the deputy yelled "Hold it!" He took a step forward, but this proved an inadequate offensive strategy.

Douglas lowered his head and barreled toward the exit to freedom, striking the deputy's stomach like a battering ram. As he covered the next thirty feet, Douglas overturned two mail carts and three citizens to delay his pursuers.

Successfully reaching his car, Douglas brought the tan Mercury to life and roared out of the parking lot onto Connecticut Street. A sharp right turn sent him northward on Ohio Route 7, but three sheriff's department cruisers were in hot pursuit.

Running the red light at Delaware Street, he raced northward, oblivious to the drops of rain that were hitting his windshield. A flash of lightning momentarily brightened the sky, and a bolt of thunder added an ominous dimension to his desperate escape.

The roadway was slickened by the new rain, and Douglas was driving far too fast for safety. Two miles north of the Old Nelson Road, where the river and the highway came within mere yards of each other, his tires slid off the pavement and the car spun a complete circle before toppling over the steep bank and into the Ohio River.

The closest cruiser saw the car leave the roadway, and braked to a stop. The two deputies ran to the riverbank.

"Not even the hood showing. We'd better call a diver."

"No time for that," replied the second deputy as he hurriedly stripped to attempt a rescue.

* * *

At one p.m. that afternoon at Greenharbor's small hospital, Tim, Martin and Lisa waited for word on Doug's condition. A medical team had been struggling to restore a heartbeat to the nearly drowned paralegal. Finally a young doctor stepped toward the vigilant part-time detectives.

"I'm sorry," he said softly. "We tried our gadgets and our shocks and our stimulant injections, but...we simply couldn't make it happen. I don't mean to sound mystic about it, but it almost seemed as if there was a test of wills going on. We wanted him back, but he wanted to die. His will was stronger."

Tim turned to the others. "Let's meet at the sheriff's office in fifteen or twenty minutes."

As Tim ambled eastward toward his destination, he realized that a haunting sadness would forever tint his thoughts and feelings of this town and this summer. There were regrets that tempered the triumphs. He regretted the net of miseries in which Douglas Grant had entangled himself. To be honest, Tim sensed how difficult it had been for Doug to live in the shadow of wealth, and yet have so little that was his own. Tim didn't hate Doug. The fifth black crow was more to be pitied than despised.

Shawn. Tim regretted how short their journey together had been. It was a relationship both happy and sad, both unusual and mundane, all rolled into one magnetic, overwhelming package. He recalled what Shawn had said, when discussing the fervor with which his mother sang spirituals. "I feel the way she did, Tim---if I ever get to the Jordan River, and hear those golden voices, I'm not turning back for no reason or *nobody*."

Eight minutes later, Tim stepped inside the county law enforcement building. As he stepped toward a group of familiar faces he noticed that Deputy Nagle had answered a phone call on one of the extensions. "No, no. Don't send anyone down here on that one. It's all closed up...old history now." Then Nagle added, as if tossing in a barely needed afterthought, "Tim Whinney solved that case."

Feeling better, Tim put his right hand on Lisa's shoulder and his left on Martin's. "There's a lot to be done. I suggest we cash in our chips here and draw a fresh hand someplace else. With hard work and diligence, we'll turn some cherished dreams into prosperous reality. Now I need to look at the Greenharbor audit report which you asked me to review."

APPENDICES AND QUESTIONS

1. Independent Auditor's Report
2. Types of Financial Audits of State and Local Governments
3. Key Terms
4. Review Questions
5. Multiple Choice Questions

Appendix 1

Bureaucrats who successfully procure an audit of inferior quality reduce the effectiveness of the audit as a monitoring device. This strategy helps to preserve the bureaucrat's control over information.
                                                    Donald R. Dies

City of Greenharbor
Independent Auditor's Report

Martin Zippa, CPA

To the Members of the City Council and Mayor
Greenharbor, Ohio:

We have audited the general purpose financial statements of the City of Greenharbor as of June 30, 199X and for the year then ended. These general purpose financial statements are the responsibility of the City's management. Our responsibility is to express an opinion on these financial statements based on our audit.

We conducted our audit in accordance with generally accepted auditing standards. Those standards require that we plan and perform the audit to obtain reasonable assurance about whether the financial statements are free of material misstatements. An audit includes examining, on a test basis, evidence supporting the amounts and disclosures in the financial statements. An audit also includes assessing the accounting principles used and significant estimates made by management, as well as evaluating the overall financial statement presentation. We believe that our audit procedures provide a reasonable basis for our opinion.

In our opinion, the general purpose financial statements referred to above represent fairly, in all material respects, and the financial position of Greenharbor City at June 30, 199X, and the results of its operations and its changes in financial position for the year ended in conformity with generally accepted accounting principles.

Martin Zippa, CPA

August 22, 199X

Appendix 2

Types of Financial Audits of State and Local Governments

A. Audits conducted under:

1. Generally accepted auditing standards

   Based on AICPA SASs and audit guides
   Applicable to all organizations

2. Generally accepted governmental auditing standards

   Based on GAO's *Government Accounting Standards* Applicable to governments and certain nonprofits

3. Single audits

   Required by Single Audit Act
   Regulations in OMB Circular A-128 for state & local governments
   Regulations in OMB Circular A-133 for nonprofits receiving federal awards

B. Additional audit requirements under GAGAS and Single audits

1. Additional working paper requirements.

2. Notification and reporting to parties other than the entity management, including the cognizant audit agency.

3 Additional reports on internal control and legal compliance at the GPFS and program levels.

4. Participant eligibility for federal financial assistance.

5. Requirements related to subrecipients (state or local government received funds which are distributed to other state or local governments or agencies, the subrecipients).

Appendix 3

Key Terms

Audit program - Written steps to be performed by the audit staff to conduct substantive testing.

Auditor's opinion - Report by the auditor stating that the financial statements have been analyzed according to GAAP and express an opinion on financial position and results of operations.

Audit standards - Auditor's professional qualifications, the quality of the audit, and the characteristics of audit reports according the AICPA or GAO requirements.

Cognizant audit agency - Federal agency assigned by OMB to carry out responsibilities under Circular A-128, including technical advice, receipt of reports in a timely fashion, and conduct quality control reviews.

Compliance testing - Testing the internal control systems to insure they are in place and working efficiently.

Engagement letter - A written agreement between the auditor and client that specifies the responsibilities of each party.

Financial audit - Examination of financial documents and other evidence to provide an auditor's opinion that the financial statements fairly present the financial position and results of operations in accordance with GAAP.

Financial and compliance audit - A financial audit plus additional compliance requirements associated with government regulations.

Generally accepted auditing standards - AICPA standards providing guidance for planning, conducting, and reporting on independent audits.

Generally accepted governmental auditing standards - GAO audit standards to provide guidance on audits to meet federal requirements.

Internal control - Accounting and administrative structures to insure proper conduct with full accountability of resources.

Performance audit - Independent determination of the effectiveness, economy, and efficiency of an organization. Performance audit criteria are specified in GAO's Yellow Book.

Preliminary planning - The initial analysis of a client's records and procedures to determine the extent of internal control evaluation and substantive testing.

Procurement - Procedures used by an organization to identify, screen, and hire an independent auditor.

Representation letter - Written response from legal counsel, attorneys general, and management on the nature of outstanding legal contingencies and other matters that could materially affect the financial position of the organization.

Request for proposal - Written request which sets forth all terms, conditions, and evaluation criteria for acquiring an audit firm.

Single audit - Federal audit requirements of state and local governments and other recipients of federal funding, conducted under (1) OMB Circular A-128 for state and local governments and (2) OMB Circular A-133 for nonprofits.

Substantive testing - Detailed analysis of the accuracy of accounting records, based on audit programs.

Systems review - An initial survey of the accounting systems in practice, used during preliminary planning to determine the extent of internal control evaluation and substantive testing.

REVIEW QUESTIONS

1. What is a financial and compliance audit?

2. How does a governmental audit compare with an audit of a commercial firm?

3. What's the difference between GAAS and GAGAS?

4. Martin conducted a systems review before he submitted a bid to audit Greenharbor. Were his procedures adequate?

5. Greenharbor's audit procurement practices were very informal. How could the procedures be improved?

6. Martin submitted a low bid, despite the possibility of fraud. Why would he do this? What are the risks involved?

7. Martin might not have detect fraud using standard audit procedures. It that a problem?

8. Martin conducted the audit during the murder investigation. What basic procedures did he perform to arrive at an opinion? What reports did he have to prepare?

9. Greenharbor received an unqualified opinion this year. Should the city have received an unqualified opinion this year?

10. If you're conducting a governmental audit what guidance (e.g., Audit Guides, SASs, regulations) would you need?

Multiple Choice Questions

1. When accounting for federal grants:

    a. An appropriate audit trail must be maintained
    b. Internal controls are not particularly important since the purpose of the audit is legal compliance
    c. The primary audit effort relates to proprietary funds according to OZW Circular 147
    d. The auditor deals exclusively with the AICPA and has no contact with the cognizant audit agency
    e. All of the above

2. The purpose of the Single Audit is:

    a. To express an opinion on the compliance with state laws for all state grants
    b. To provide a uniform audit approach and documentation procedures for financial and compliance audits
    c. To insure that financial reports are presented in accordance with state and federal laws
    d. All of the above
    e. None of the above

3. The primary source of generally accepted auditing standards for governmental units is:

    a. Statements on Auditing Standards issued by the Auditing Standards Board of the AIGPA
    b. GASB and NCGA standards
    c. GASB and FASB standards
    d. Single Audit Act and NCGA standards
    e. All of the above

4. The basic audit of a state or local government is called:

    a. The legal and program compliance audit
    b. Internal control and assessment testing
    c. The financial and compliance audit
    d. Specific programs audit
    e. Cognizant audit agency audit

5. The Single Audit Act requires the following report(s) or schedule(s):

    a. Auditor's opinion
    b. Schedule of Federal financial assistance
    c. Report on internal accounting controls
    d. Report on compliance with Federal laws and regulations
    e. All of the above

6. The source of generally accepted governmental auditing standards (GAGAS) is:

    a. The GAO's Yellow Book, Government Auditing Standards
    b. Statements on auditing standards issued by the Auditing Standards Board
    c. The AICPA's Audit Guide, Audits of State and Local Governmental Units
    d. Statements issued by the Government Accounting Standards Board

7. A local government receiving $10,000 in Federal financial assistance is:

    a. Required to have a single audit
    b. Exempt from single audit requirements
    c. Must have either a single audit or a series of separate grant audits
    d. Must be audited by the General Accounting Office
    e. None of the above

8. The auditor's report includes:

    a. An explanatory paragraph on supplemental unaudited information
    b. The opinion paragraph
    c. A scope paragraph
    d. A paragraph describing the responsibilities of the auditor and the management of the client firm
    e. All of the above

9. Major weaknesses in internal control and material noncompliance with federal regulations require written reports from the auditor to:

   a. The public in the comprehensive annual financial report
   b. Applicable government officials and cognizant audit agencies
   c. General Accounting Office
   d. The state auditor and state board of public accountancy
   e. All of the above

10. The engagement letter should include:

    a. The nature of the engagement
    b. Type of audit
    c. Scope of the audit
    d. Use of client's staff
    e. All of the above

11. Tracing a random sample of properties from a city map to the assessment rolls would be an example of:

    a. Systems review
    b. Substantive testing
    c. Evaluation of internal control
    d. Program compliance auditing
    e. None of the above

12. The purpose of compliance testing is:

    a. To provide a basis to conclude if internal controls are being applied as prescribed
    b. To provide a basis for the determination of the appropriate audit fee
    c. To test efficiency as part of a performance audit
    d. To determine if financial statements are prepared according to GAAP, but only if federal financial assistance is greater than $100,000
    e. All of the above

13. Cognizant audit agencies:

   a. Are federal agencies that establish audit regulations
   b. Are specific federal agencies that are assigned audit responsibilities for particular state and local governments
   c. Are state agencies with the authority to conduct single audits
   d. Are CPA firms that are licensed specifically to do single audits
   e. None of the above